HOW TO
SELL WHAT YOU

Tradeoffs
Making Good
Women on Top
Sex and the Single Parent
The Promised Land *(a play)*

HOW TO
SELL WHAT YOU

JANE ADAMS

G. P. PUTNAM'S SONS / NEW YORK

Designed by Richard Oriolo

Library of Congress Cataloging in Publication Data

Adams, Jane.
How to sell what you write.

1. Authorship. I. Title.
PN161.A3   1984   808'.02   84-4871
ISBN 0-399-12982-0

Printed in the United States of America

To Toby, who showed me the beginning

CONTENTS

DO YOU REALLY WANT
TO WRITE?

This book is not about how to write; if you are a writer, published or not, you already know how to do that. It is about selling what you write, an entirely different matter.

I am not talking about great writing, which is Art, but about the kind of writing that can be learned and practiced and used to create a work that gets published. It may never win a Pulitzer Prize or top the best-seller list or generate great critical acclaim, but it can put money in your pocket, enhance your reputation, and nourish your ego.

I am talking about Craft, which is different from Art. Certainly, the more Art there is in your Craft, the better your writing will be. However, that may not make it easier to sell.

There are some writers who are deadly serious about their Art, and, by chance or inclination, remain above the unaesthetic business of selling their work and far removed from the industry of publishing. Occasionally talent prevails over obscurity if someone closer to the real world happens along, recognizes the intrinsic quality or commercial appeal of the work, and helps the writer get it published. If the writer is extremely fortunate, money or even fame follows. That's the hard way.

There is an easier way, and this book tells you what it is. It has only a remote connection with Art, which may be a sad commentary on the state of publishing, or public taste, today. There is a truism which bears repeating here: Art, like beauty, is its own excuse for being. Any publisher worth his backlist would agree. But just look at his current titles and it is evident that many books that have nothing to do with Art sell quite briskly. Would a Serious Artist have anything to do with thin thighs, dead cats, or G-Spots?

Perhaps not. But a professional writer might, someone who understands that making a living or even some extra money from writing requires treating it as a Craft—in fact, as a business.

Writing is a solitary vocation, requiring only your chosen instrument—pen, typewriter, or word processor—plus an act of imagination, a facility with language, and the talent to combine them. Selling is an interpersonal transaction that requires finding a Buyer and convincing him or her to buy your Product. Many writers have no idea how to do this, and some have no inclination to learn. If you are among those without inclination and are not fortunate enough to have been born of a wealthy family, plan to marry into one. If you think selling your writing as if it were soap or insurance demeaning, this book is not for you. Put it back on the shelf right now—or, better yet, buy it for a hungry writer you know. Then go to the Great Literature department and enjoy yourself.

If you sincerely want to sell what you write, read on.

First, the good news. Writing is an honorable profession. At best it *is* Art, at worst it harms no one. The process teaches you what you need to learn, the hours are good, and you can stare out of your window for long periods of time and still tell people, truthfully, that you are working.

The bad news is that (a) being a writer is like always having homework, and (b) even if you sell consistently, you may still have to find other work to support your writing habit, earnings being what they are these days in publishing. In fact, the odds that you will earn more than a poverty-level income as a full-time writer are low. A recent survey indicated that less than five percent of writers who had books published within the last two years earned more than five thousand dollars for their work. Many book writers supplement their advances or royalties with magazine fees, if they can. And many film writers give up and go back to the feed store in Iowa every year.

But selling what you write is not impossible. Neither is earning a living from your work. It can be done. There are some very successful writers whose work seems to sell itself. They can command extraordinary sums for a few words scribbled on a napkin at the Four Seasons, where publishers wine, dine, and pay them the world for that simple outline of their next project. But in the beginning they starved too.

For you and me, every sale is the culmination of more than just a great idea. It is the end product of a process that involved creating not only a work, but also a sales strategy and a marketing package. For those of us who are not publishing superstars, writing is only part of the process; the rest is selling.

Norman Mailer once described a professional writer as someone who could write on a bad day. Substitute "sell" for "write" and you have a more complete job description. Selling involves compromise. Sometimes it is a compromise between Art and Commerce. Sometimes it is between what you want to write and what you must write to make a sale. Often it requires adapting, revising, or rewriting in order to meet a specific market, formula, genre, or editorial or production demand. Often you have to put an idea or a manuscript away until you can find the right editor, publisher, or agent, or until you can generate sufficient interest in it as written or proposed. That's what selling is about, and this book tells you how to do it.

Most writers do not think of their work or their words as a Product, of the process involved in getting it published as Marketing, or of publishers, editors, producers, and (sometimes) agents as Buyers. Nor do they think of their readers as Customers. As a writer, you may have a hazy idea of who will buy your book or read your article besides your family, friends, and fifth-grade teacher. That idea may be wildly inaccurate, but even if it isn't, you may be overlooking the important distinction between your reader and your Buyer. And if you cannot reach and sell to a Buyer, your work will never get to its readers—your Customers.

The more you understand about the basic techniques of marketing and are able to apply them to your writing, the less frequently you will need to wait on tables, teach English, or write advertising copy. If that last job is what you're doing now to support your Muse, however, you're several steps ahead in the process of learning to sell what you write. My experience for a decade as a copywriter for several ad agencies and as the sole proprietor of my own agency taught me how to market products. It also taught me that the same principles that apply to selling cornflakes, soap, or cosmetics can be effectively employed in selling what I write.

In the seven years since I last wrote ad copy I've sold more than a hundred magazine and newspaper articles, four nonfiction books, two novels, and a full-length play. One of my books was made into a television movie and another was optioned for a series. None of the articles or books was entirely written before it was sold; my first novel was sold with a sample, outline, and proposal.

My first book began as a newspaper article, was ex-

panded into a book, diversified into several magazine articles, was adapted and sold to Hollywood, and launched
me into an additional career as a lecturer and teacher. As
one idea became several Products, I began to understand
that there is a big difference between writing and publishing and that the connection between them is marketing.
When I began to approach my writing like a marketer, I
became a consistently selling writer.

What I've been telling you, and what is in the following
pages, is what I teach the students in my "How to Sell
What You Write" seminars, given all over the country.
And it's at just about this point in the seminars that some
Serious Artist in the group inquires whether that isn't
being a "huckster." In other words, can't writers have
ethics and values?

Certainly they can. In fact, they must. To write simply
because the market will buy is not reason enough; if it is
the only justification, the writing will inevitably be the
poorer for it. Writers must exercise personal choice, not
only of words and phrases but of subjects and emphases,
too. If they do not have concern and compassion for what
they write, no one will want to read it.

Writing can be a hobby, an avocation, a supplemental
vocation, or a career. It has been all those things to me.
With my first byline it became my identity and my ambi-
tion. I had no career plan, but with my first sale my goal
became focused: to write whatever I felt like writing—an
article, a book, an essay, a play—and get paid for it, get
paid enough so that I would never have to do anything
else for a living. That's what I began to plan for, and
eventually it happened. You may make a number of sales
before you realize that what you have, along with several
clippings or even a book, is a career as a writer. Or that
may be your goal from the start. I say the sooner the
better, and hope this book helps you start thinking along
those lines.

I also hope it will help you think of yourself as a professional and that it will direct you to sources that can help with your specific marketing problem and suggest ways to package your work to attract the right Buyers, as I do in my seminars. Many of my students had been writing for a long time and never sold a single piece of their work. Many now do so, over and over again. And if you can write worth a damn, so can you.

THE THEORY OF
LOOKING BACKWARD

The publishing industry, in magazines as well as books, has undergone severe change and disruption in recent years. The state of the national economy, advances in technology, and competition from other information and entertainment media have contributed to this change, and so have factors in the industry itself, from the fluctuating cost of paper to changes in business and accounting practices made when large conglomerates moved into publishing. Some critics blame the decline in publishing profits on the increasing market share captured by the large chain stores and discounters; those who follow magazines attribute the disappearance of many well-known mastheads from magazine racks to the rise in postage costs.

The change that has had the greatest impact on writers is the trend known as narrowcasting—publishing for definable market segments rather than for a mass audience. While this is most clearly indicated in magazines, it has had an effect on book publishing and film production, too. In what John Naisbitt, author of *Megatrends,* calls the "multiple option" society, the either/or choices of earlier times have given way to an explosion of diversity, which means that consumers, in this case readers, may and must be pursued market by market. "In a relatively short time, the unified mass society has fractionalized into many diverse groups of people with a wide array of differing tastes and values, what advertisers call a market-segmented, market-decentralized society," he writes.

This fact has tremendous influence on trade book as well as magazine publishing today. And while it is not necessary to be an expert on every aspect of the publishing industry in order to sell what you write, it *is* essential to know everything you can about the environment in which your Products must compete in order to market them successfully. You wouldn't try to sell cars without knowing something about what happens in Detroit (or Tokyo, for that matter) or about the economics of automobile production and distribution, and you shouldn't try to sell your writing without some background on the industry of publishing, either. Which brings us to the Theory of Looking Backward.

A MARKETING TECHNIQUE THAT WORKS

The marketing rules I apply to selling what I write are those I learned in the advertising business. Good advertising (advertising that sells products) and good writing (writing that is publication-worthy) have this in common: Both must tell a story clearly, concisely, and creatively. That, by the way, is one of the few basic rules of writing included in this book. If you can't do this, it's time to reconsider your chosen lifework.

Other parallels between selling advertising and selling writing are easiest to illustrate if we adapt the language of marketing to that of publishing. Thus the book, article, or script becomes your Product, the reader becomes your

Customer, and your Buyer—the publisher, editor, producer, or agent to whom you must sell your Product—is the link between them. The same three requirements for a marketing campaign apply to the business of selling your writing. Read them, memorize them, and don't forget them:

1. Know your Buyer *and* your Customer.
2. Understand their *separate* needs and problems.
3. Provide a Product that *answers* their needs and problems.

Stan Soderberg, who taught me those rules, also taught me the Theory of Looking Backward, which is what he used in approaching every account his advertising agency handled. You can and should apply it to every Product you create.

The Theory of Looking Backward, in essence, is this: Nothing happens until somebody sells something. Applied to advertising, the theory starts at the point of sale and moves backward, conceptually and practically, to the creation of the ads. A good campaign starts by considering the Customer's problems, habits, and methods of purchase. It then considers those same factors as they apply to the Buyer—in agency terms, the client. With this information, a marketing campaign is created that often includes adapting the Product or its packaging to answer the needs and problems of Buyer and Customer.

Using the Theory of Looking Backward, you can examine an existing Product (a manuscript) and determine a marketing strategy (a package) appropriate to it, whose object is to convince a Buyer that the Product addresses his needs and problems. Inside that package, of course, are your words, and once you've interested your Buyer, they must be as good as you say they are.

The process will work when applied to a completed manuscript. But it's much easier to put into practice before that point, when an idea is still in the outline stage—in fact, before you've written a word. This saves a great deal of rewriting later.

While I was still writing copy for Stan Soderberg's advertising agency, I put the Theory of Looking Backward into my own freelance writing. By adapting the techniques of marketing commodities to those of selling my writing, I presold my first book. It began with a proposal for a newspaper article titled "Sex and the Single Parent." I identified the Customer (the eventual reader) and the appropriate Buyer (a weekly newspaper). The Customer needed information on how to deal with an increasingly prevalent, thorny personal problem; the Buyer needed to balance hard investigative reporting with occasional "soft" cover stories, and had a problem attracting the educated middle-class audience to which his publication was addressed.

I understood the Customer because I was one myself, so it was easy to start from the point of sale—the Customer seeing the newspaper on the stands—and work backward to create a Product that would also meet the needs of the Buyer. I identified a quantifiable population affected by the subject, which dovetailed with the newspaper's demographics, and included enough statistics and data on both Customer and Buyer (divorce figures and the magazine's reader profile) to add weight to my proposal. Finally, I had an outline of the article. No sample was necessary because I had written for the newspaper before and was, in fact, a contributing editor.

When an agent approached me about expanding my article into a book (yes, sometimes it happens that way, but not often!), I undertook the same kind of analysis. The published article served as a sample along with a detailed chapter outline. That became the Product. If the Buyer had been, say, an academic publisher, I would have prepared a different outline and Product. But because it was addressed to the same Customer as the article had been, only in a national rather than a regional market, I changed only the data and statistics. I added a review of existing literature, both popular and academic, which pointed out that there were no competing books on the subject, although it had been covered in parts of some books about divorce that had performed well in the market.

Perhaps none of the information included in my proposal was news to my Buyer, but it did prove my awareness of his needs and problems and of a market that existed for the Product. And in the third incarnation of *Sex and the Single Parent,* as a television movie, that same material told the Buyer (a producer) and the Customer (the network that bought the movie) the same things, and was used to create the Product (the film) and advertise it.

Looking backward helps the Buyer focus on his Customer and suggests a strategy for reaching him. It is never presumptuous to do this for a Buyer, particularly a publisher. Many writers believe that only publishers know what will sell and to whom; if this were true, there would be no remainder houses and no unsold inventory in publishers' warehouses.

The Theory of Looking Backward is not infallible; in publishing, as in most industries, there are no rules that are never broken. That is certainly true of marketing. The Theory of Looking Backward does not explain, for instance, why millions of people bought books about dead cats. But one particular aspect of the theory is important—indeed, essential—to every Product you create, before or after you create it. Put yourself in the position of your Buyer as well as your Customer and give him what he needs and therefore what he wants.

HOW ABOUT FICTION?

It's much easier to apply the Theory of Looking Backward to nonfiction than to fiction, since today's cultural diversity means that there is a segment of the market available for a decently written article or book on almost every subject. And it is easier to break into the nonfiction market because it is easier to identify by some demographic measurement the number of people who might be interested in a subject. Nonfiction is also easier to sell before it is completely written; often a sale can be made on the basis of a good outline and proposal. For all but superstar writers, though, fiction is a risky business, and it is almost impossible to find a Buyer who will purchase it without at least a complete first draft. There are exceptions to this rule: Category fiction is frequently sold without a completed manuscript, and a strong writing sample can sell an incomplete novel if the subject is deemed highly commercial or if a writer has strong credits in another area. That happened to me. The subject of my first novel was one I had treated in previous nonfiction books, and there was an identifiable market, growing in size and purchasing power, for novels about women and success, the subject of *Tradeoffs*. Finally, it is much easier to sell nonfiction without an agent. If you don't have a personal relationship with a Buyer and don't have an agent to bridge the gap, noncategory fiction is a very tough sale.

There are ways to initiate relationships with Buyers, even (and usually) by mail, and they work even if your second cousin isn't the secretary to a publisher or your best friend isn't an agent (almost nobody's is). It is not impossible to get your fiction seen by or sold to a publisher without an agent. Techniques like the Theory of Looking Backward, while specifically designed for nonfiction writers, can also help novelists. Fiction reflects the interests and concerns of the reading public, just as nonfiction explicates them. Even so-called literary fiction appeals to a Buyer when it addresses the universal human concerns of Customers, although it may be purely imaginary and seem irrelevant to daily life or purely escapist in subject matter.

Many writers I know, including journalists, teachers, and copywriters, have fantasies about publishing a novel.

Even those who regularly sell nonfiction realize how difficult it is to fulfill that fantasy. They know how the cost of publishing blockbuster novels has made necessary the use of money otherwise available for experimental fiction or even an adequate traditional novel, despite publishers' protests to the contrary. In fact, it often seems that everything from fickle taste to the state of the economy conspires against novelists. It took me dozens of sales to periodicals and three nonfiction books just to get an agent to look at the outline of a novel. And what helped me sell that was everything I had learned from selling nonfiction, and everything I knew about marketing.

So if you're a fiction writer, don't skip the pages that appear to be of interest only to nonfiction writers. They may seem irrelevant to your writing, but they are very relevant to your selling. And if you'd like to eat more regularly while waiting for someone to discover the great novel in you, consider using your talents to write and sell nonfiction. It will not only sustain you financially and hone your craft, but it will also bring you into closer contact with Customers and Buyers and help you get your fiction seen, sold, and read.

3

GETTING TO KNOW
YOUR BUSINESS

The first step in every marketing campaign is information gathering. You need to learn everything you can about the business, the market, and the product. The business is the publishing industry. The market is wherever people buy books or magazines or see films. (Although this book is primarily addressed to writers of books and articles, its points also apply to scriptwriters for screen, stage, or radio, so just adapt the language of your environment to what comes next.) And the Product is the total of all the books and magazines available for sale. If you begin at the point of purchase—remember the Theory of Looking Backward—your first, last, and most frequent stop will be the bookstore.

THE IMPORTANCE
OF BOOKSTORES
IN A WRITER'S LIFE

Many writers who come to my seminars or private selling conferences spend very little time in bookstores, and their most typical explanation is that they cannot afford to. This amazes me—the last time I looked, no bookstore charged admission. Buying is only one reason for a writer to go to a bookstore; not being able to buy is no reason not to spend as much time as you can in as many different bookstores as you can find. You go to watch what happens at the point of sale, to watch the transaction and all the attendant activity close up. You go to see what books customers pick up, replace, or purchase. You go to get a sense of the excitement that some Products do or do not generate in customers. You go to see what is out there and how it differs from or is like your own work. You go to collect data; you go to nourish your Muse. Most of all you go for the following reason: *If you don't know what sells, you can't sell what you write.*

You go to bookstores to learn what is successful in publishing so that you can take advantage of that knowledge in your own work. Remember, most publishers prefer not to tamper with what has been successful for them in the past, especially since they're usually not certain exactly why a particular book was a success. This is equally true of magazine publishers and movie and television producers, which is why many books are derivative, most magazine articles strike you as having been printed before, most movies and television series are like other movies and series, and why trends seem to sweep the publishing and film industries at the same time, or nearly so.

In bookstores, stock changes several times a week (daily in big stores). You can see it happen when you frequent them. You rarely notice this process in a library, for which there is also a place in every writer's life—more about that later. A bookstore is where you begin to cultivate a feel for changes in publishing trends and buying habits. For a selling writer, that feel is essential, as it is for any professional in any industry. Television executive Roone Arledge, for instance, is said to have "the feel" in his business; he describes it as a sense of what people are interested in, "being not too far ahead and not too far behind the public." For writers, a bookstore is the first and best place to cultivate the feel.

Each bookstore has its own personality, its own customer mix, its own proprietor's preferences, which are reflected in the books offered for sale. If you are writing a travel book, you should find a travel bookstore; if you are writing a business book, you should look for that kind of specialty bookstore; if you are a science fiction writer, you should stake out the shops that cater to those readers—your Customers. When you visit a bookstore to see what is available that is like your Product, spend as much time as you can in the appropriate department. A good large chain store will have some of what's available in a given category, but a specialty bookstore will have all of it, as well as an owner or manager who knows that particular publishing market better than the manager of a general-interest bookstore. Make it a point to visit all the stores in your area regularly, and to shop the specialty bookstores in large cities. If you've just written *Buy God: Praying Your Way to Wealth,** you should know every religious bookstore in your region and have catalogs from the ones outside of it. If you're trying to write *Co-Op Shopping Can Save You Money,* you should be familiar with the alternative bookstores, university bookstores, or even the food co-ops, which typically carry books like yours. And if the subject of your book makes it appropriate for non-

---

*This book is a fictitious example: If you don't know which other titles I mention are real, you're not spending enough time in the market.

bookstore outlets, you must watch what happens at these points of sale as well.

When you browse in a bookstore, watch, listen, and learn. The store manager or assistant or a well-informed clerk can be a major resource in your education. Sometimes you can eavesdrop as a Buyer meets with a Seller— as the store manager works with a publisher's sales representative. Observing that act of selling by individually negotiating for each Product can demonstrate graphically how books are marketed. In *In Cold Type: Overcoming the Book Crisis,* Leonard Shatzkin gives an excellent portrayal of this transaction, but nothing substitutes for watching it happen yourself. Sometimes a bookseller whose friendship you have cultivated will introduce you to a sales rep, who may help you get your manuscript to an editor at his company. Some book reps get finders' fees for bringing new authors into a house; others are editorially very sophisticated, have close relationships with senior editors or sales managers (who wield a great deal of power in the selection of Products), and may be able to sell your Product for you.

You may not be a big spender at your local bookstore, but your enthusiasm for books will be noted and remembered by the sales people when you come in regularly and make at least occasional purchases. No matter how geographically remote you are from the publishing industry, its best expression is in a bookstore, and there is at least one in your community. Be sure to visit bookstores in other cities when you travel; sometimes differences in regional market buying habits are apparent just from the differences in book stock.

LEARNING THE TRADE AT THE LIBRARY

You may not have a big budget for books and magazines—and with today's prices you need one—but some reference books should be consulted when formulating your marketing plan, and that's what libraries are for.

Literary Market Place and *Publishers Weekly* are not readily available in most bookstores, but they are required reading for the professional writer and can usually be found in libraries. *LMP* is the basic reference directory for everyone in the business from publishers to agents; it's a *Who's Who* of your Buyers and of services you may need in the preparation as well as the marketing of your Products.

PW is the weekly bible of the industry. It is useful not only for reviews of forthcoming books, but also for news, analyses, and trends in publishing. What kinds of books are selling, which editors are moving to new houses, who paid what for a paperback sale, what's new in religious books, how romance lines are multiplying—it's all in *PW* every week, and some bit of information may be just what you need to direct your Product to a specific Buyer, adapt it to meet a stated need, or revise it as you see what it's competing against. An article in *PW* about an agent who specializes in computer books led one of my writers right to the person he was looking for. Another article about the softening market for westerns helped another writer rethink the category book he was having trouble selling. One novelist who had written a love story with strong religious overtones read in *PW* about a new line of inspirational romances, which had not yet appeared in the bookstores; within weeks, she had made a positive contact with a Buyer.

You should read *PW* regularly, whether you subscribe to it or get it at the library. Also at the library, check out the *Publishers Weekly Yearbook,* which summarizes trends and news of the previous year, or *PW*'s occasional index to reviews of recent publications. There may be market data or directions to beef up your marketing plan. And keeping up with the trade press helps you understand how the industry works. At first, much of what you read may sound like a foreign language, but soon you'll catch on and know what's meant by rights, permissions, advances, reorders, backlists. You'll learn which houses are expanding and which are cutting back their lists. You'll see how new technological developments affect what is published and what is sold. A selected list of writers' reference materials is also included at the end of this chapter to guide you in the information-gathering process.

Changes in the top management of big publishers occasionally make the newspapers, but in the trade press you'll get the kind of detail that can help you identify just the right Buyer for your Product. If, for example, you've just finished outlining *Eating Your Way to Higher Consciousness: The New Age Vegetarian Cookbook* and you note a story in *PW* about a publisher launching an independent line of nonfiction books on popular health, spirituality, and cooking (J.P. Tarcher, Inc.), you'll have your manuscript on his desk this week . . . won't you?

Don't neglect any source of information about your industry, your Buyer, and your Customer. Read the trade press regularly. And if you're writing in a particular category, become familiar with the publications of that segment of the publishing market, too; from the *Script Writer's Marketplace* to the Poets & Writers newsletter, there's a publication that can help put you in touch with your market. Most of these are listed in various sections of *LMP,* but a friendly librarian can probably provide information as well. Identify these special resources and use them to bridge the time gap in information gathered by watching the daily or weekly flow of books and magazines in and out of retail outlets, since the trade press reports on what will be happening in the near future as well as what has recently occurred in the industry.

Most writers work in isolation, and during the creation of the Product, that's necessary. In the work's final stages—that time when you write just to get it out of your head so you can sleep—it's essential. But when you are conceptualizing a Product or casting around for an idea for one, making contact with your industry is very useful. You make that contact in the bookstore and in the library, and especially in the trade press.

ESTABLISHING A COMMUNITY OF COLLEAGUES

Another source of information about the publishing industry is writers—people who do what you do and sell to the same markets. I've found most writers to be generous with their contacts and helpful in introducing other writers to their agents, editors, and publishers. It's important for you to have a sense of what your colleagues are doing, and if there is no literary community in your area, you may have to establish one by seeking out other writers. Often a university or a local newspaper or magazine is the core of a group like this. So, too, are writers' conferences and organizations. Outside of New York and a few other large cities, we do not have the networks that other industries do. But networking, a new-age term for trading names and connections, can go on wherever two writers or a writer and a Buyer meet—at bookstores, in creative writing courses, in conferences, and in the trade press. Contacts are as important to a writer as his words; they can sometimes make the difference between getting your work in front of a Buyer or having it languish, unread, in his slush pile.

Writers who attend my seminars usually leave with a list of addresses and the telephone numbers of the rest of the group. Until then, they have not easily made contact with their peers. Perhaps that is because they feel vulnerable and/or envious in the company of those who have published more frequently than they have. Or it may be because writing is, after all, a solitary pursuit. But the time you spend away from your desk meeting new people who are in the same business is also work time and it is very important. It keeps your awareness current, your antennae out for a useful name or contact, and it hones your sense of what's happening in the writing world.

If you know anyone who writes and publishes regularly,

get to know him or her better. Aggressively seek out others who understand how the business works. This lessens your isolation somewhat, and it can also spark new ideas and possibilities.

Many writers band together in support groups. They read and criticize each other's work, share their contacts, and provide help to newcomers. In large cities these organizations may advertise widely. In smaller cities, you'll have to seek and find your own affinity groups. Some of you may already have what other writers want and need—an agent, an editor, a connection. I urge you to be generous about sharing that information with other writers, depending on how your agent or editor feels about unsolicited referrals. On a bad day, when your typewriter won't talk to you and you need someone who will, it's nice to have a colleague you can call.

So go out and network. At the national level there are organizations like the Authors Guild, Poets & Writers, PEN, and the American Society of Journalists and Authors, which provide useful information and services like ASJA's Dial-A-Writer. Some are open only to members, and some have requirements for membership. For names and addresses of organizations in your field, check the *Directory of Associations,* which can be found in any library.

Writers' conferences have no requirement for admission and in every region of the nation there is at least one held annually. At these events, Buyers—editors, publishers, and agents—look for talented writers and commercial properties. The May issue of *The Writer* and *LMP* have comprehensive listings of established conferences, which can be invaluable for making connections that will help you sell your work. Do not be put off by the long line of aspiring authors waiting to talk to a Buyer. And when you reach the head of the line, also do not be pushy or demand that he read and critique your manuscript immediately. Ask instead if you may send him your work or your proposal. Ask for a business card if the opportunity presents itself. Even if you have nothing to show a Buyer now, write him within a week of the contact to reintroduce yourself and explain that you hope to have something to submit soon, or ask any relevant questions that were not answered in your (however brief) meeting or in the speech he gave. Remind him of your meeting at the start of the letter; repeat in a few brief sentences your area of interest or work. Thank him for his attention, too. By establishing a relationship via the mail, you may get to the point where he solicits you for a submission, or at least remembers you when your proposal or work arrives.

Every publisher, editor, and agent depends for a living, ultimately, on the writer. Which is why you should never pass up an opportunity to make a connection with a potential Buyer. And neither should you miss a chance to talk to a published writer, especially one whose area is similar to yours. Some will tell you whatever they know. A few will offer to introduce you by mail to their own agents or editors. Just being able to write to a Buyer with some version of "John Doe, your author, suggested I send you the enclosed proposal" puts you one up on the person who mails off a manuscript to a stranger or, worse, to an unnamed person—"Editor in Chief, Flim Flam Press," for example—who has no reason to read beyond your first page. Unless, of course, that first page is brilliant, riveting, and reads like money in the bank. (More about how to accomplish *that* later.)

The publishing business often seems like a private club, but in fact it is not. It is an industry, and without a Product—yours or someone else's—it has no reason to exist. Familiarizing yourself with it and getting a feel for the market is part of the research you must do to become a consistently selling writer. Staying current with both should be a regular part of your professional agenda.

READING, READING, AND MORE READING

Another equally essential element of research is reading. Read every single thing you can find that is in any way like what you are writing. That is working. Reading for pleasure is leisure, and in most cases it will improve your writing, but reading for comparison is part of the data collection process that is central to your proposal to a Buyer. If you are writing a category novel, for instance, read every single one you can find in that category—the bad ones as well as the good. The best way to learn what works is to see what doesn't. The only way to know how your work is different from what is already available is to know what's in print. If you're preparing a nonfiction proposal, it is central to the proposal's worth that you be able to identify other books on similar subjects and indicate how yours is different or similar. Remember, publishers *are* imitative, so telling a Buyer "There's never been anything like my book" is likely to evoke as a response some variation of "And there's probably a very good reason for that."

Many writers who come to my seminars report that they avoid reading work similar to their own, or, even if they don't, that they avoid comparing their work with that of other writers. That is patently ridiculous. Once again, if you don't know what's selling, you can't sell what you write. Some of those stubborn writers have told me that they don't want their work "contaminated" by reading similar writing. A phrase I often hear (but not from regularly selling writers) is "I'm afraid I'll lose my individual voice." That's ridiculous, too. If you are lucky enough to have a voice or a tone or a style, you won't lose it by exposing it to the work of other authors. Reading their work may only reinforce your faith in your own or indicate ways in which you can improve it.

Take the best (and bestselling) variation on your own

theme and look up reviews of the work. Find out, if you can, how well the book sold. Determine who edited it and who the agent was—often you can learn this simply by calling the publisher. Occasionally, too, this information is included in the author's acknowledgments or dedication. If your work is really as good or better than what you've read, with a strong proposal or sample you may be able to convince a Buyer to consider it.

None of this is meant to imply that your work should copy something already in print. But to the extent that you can indicate how your work is similar or related to what has already been profitable for a Buyer, you're helping him solve a problem—namely, what is this material like, and how can I categorize it for my sales force or Customers? There is derivation, there is slavish imitation, and there is plagiarism; you as a writer know, or should know, the differences.

CULTIVATING PROFESSIONAL READING HABITS

Every writer's personal library includes a dictionary, a thesaurus, and probably a dog-eared copy of Bartlett's *Familiar Quotations*. Depending on your area of interest, you may own or have access to other reference books, too. This is the list of references I use most often:

Encyclopedia of Associations (Gale Research, Detroit).

Literary Market Place (R. R. Bowker, New York).

Magazine Industry Market Place (R. R. Bowker, New York).

Publishers' Trade List Annual (R. R. Bowker, New York), contains catalogs from publishers.

Readers' Guide to Periodical Literature (H. W. Wilson, New York).

Research Centers Directory (Gale Research, Detroit).

Standard Periodical Directory (Oxbridge Communications, New York).
Statistical Abstract of the U.S. Government Printing Office (Washington, DC).
Statistics Sources (Gale Research, Detroit).
Subject Guide to Books in Print and *Subject Guide to Forthcoming Books* (R. R. Bowker, New York).

These are industry and market materials with which you should be familiar:

Authors Guild Bulletin (Authors Guild, 234 W. 44th St., New York, NY 10036).
Coda: Poets & Writers Newsletter (Poets & Writers, 201 W. 54th St., New York, NY 10019).
Fiction Writer's Market (Writer's Digest Books, Cincinnati).
International Directory of Little Magazines & Small Presses (Dustbooks, Paradise, CA).
Publishers Weekly (R. R. Bowker, New York).
The Writer (8 Arlington Street, Boston, MA).
Writer's Market (Writer's Digest Books, Cincinnati).

TUNING INTO THE
INFORMATION OZONE

With an understanding of the industry, a sense of what transpires at the point of purchase, and a familiarity with competing products in the marketplace, you are ready to begin creating a marketing plan—to consider what you know and can write that will sell because there is a need for it and thus a Customer and a Buyer who will benefit from it. Even before you've settled on the right medium for your idea—fiction, nonfiction, script, or whatever—you must fix in your mind a clear picture of who will be interested in what you have to say.

THE PET ROCK
THEORY

I almost never put paper in my typewriter until my creative idea is well developed enough to plan how to market it. Some people have called this the Pet Rock Theory of writing. They are also the people who characterize as Art only those expressions that spring from a nobler, or more obscure, source. May they all find a Buyer who cares more for art than profit. Meanwhile, my suggestion is to employ the Pet Rock Theory: Be first with a creative idea that's also commercial. Of course, being second or seventy-second with a better or more creatively realized version of an idea—especially in nonfiction—doesn't automatically disqualify you. Once again, publishing is an imitative business, and there are trends that do determine what is bought and what is not. But spotting those trends first is better. Just ask the millionaire who dreamed up the Pet Rock.

CAN I USE THIS?

Waiting for the Muse to come to you is chancy. By the time she shows up at your desk you may have been driven into the world of regular jobs. So don't sit around waiting for creative inspiration to strike; cultivate a habit of mind that provides fertile soil for ideas to burrow into. Briefly, that means evaluating everything you read, see, hear, or experience for its utilitarian value. Learn to ask yourself this question: Can I use this?

Is there a story, article, film in what you know or can learn? Is there an angle, a twist, a style that could turn this into an idea, and then into a Product? Is there a market for this material or information, and can you shape it into something salable?

That habit of mind is called curiosity, and it is a selling writer's most useful asset. It's what helps a writer be first to spot a trend, a new need, a potential market. It's what tunes you into the Information Ozone.

The Information Ozone is my name for all the facts, figures, sources, and data out there waiting for someone to use them to make a point or create a marketable Product. Sometimes the Information Ozone seems random—a phrase or story or fact that happens to flit across your personal information screen. Other times it comes from a determined screening of all possible sources of data. The best source of printed matter in the Information Ozone is the regular reading of newspapers and periodicals. A professional writer should read at least two newspapers daily—a good national paper and a regional or local newspaper. The latter should be included not because you write on regional subjects or sell to regional markets, but because a regular sampling of these periodicals provides clues to what is important around the country, and national papers often miss a small story ·that hints at the beginning of a trend with wider implications. This is my prescription for regular reading, especially for a nonfiction writer:

Daily:
- *The New York Times*
- One local newspaper
- One regional newspaper from another part of the country
- *The Wall Street Journal* or *USA Today*

Weekly:
- *Publishers Weekly*
- One book review
- One news magazine

Monthly:
- One writer's magazine
- One special-interest periodical
- Every magazine you've ever sold to or want to sell to
- One consumer magazine in a new field

As *Megatrends* author John Naisbitt points out, trends are generated from the bottom up. He bases the findings about society's future directions outlined in his book on an analysis of millions of articles about local events in America's towns and cities during the past twelve years.

For writers with personal computers, the Information Ozone is as close as your data base, which can bring information about any conceivable subject directly to you. The computerized bulletin-board systems that serve as information networks for computer owners also offer a clear picture of what many people are thinking and talking about and of special interests and the markets that serve them. Dialog Information Retrieval Service, for example, offers more than 180 data bases, from magazine and newspaper indexes to individual topics—eighty million entries in all.

The Information Ozone has printed sources, ranging from the *Census Bureau Abstract* to these computer bulletin boards, and it includes all media. In level of sophistication it can be as wispy as a fragment of a conversation overheard at a party or as solid as an electronic data base. By filtering the ozone through your own screen (that market feel you've begun to cultivate) you can start to sort and catalog what you know that might interest Buyers and Customers. An interest in the world around you, in the ways that people see and experience that world and how they think, feel, act, and live is important whether you write fiction or nonfiction. So is your willingness to make everything that happens to you and to people you know grist for your writer's mill.

WHERE IDEAS COME FROM

You don't need a computer to tap into the Information Ozone, although it helps. If you are a regular and attentive reader, if you're involved with people, easy to talk to, and are naturally curious, you can create your own information sources, and the start of a creative idea will come from them. Sometimes a fragment of an article can spark an idea. In my seminars the group often scans a daily newspaper to practice turning ideas into Products. A piece about a computer camp, for example, sparked these ideas among one group: a book listing all special-interest adult camps from tennis to cooking, with complete information on each one and a regional cross-index; an article for *Cosmopolitan* about finding romance at such a camp; a movie with an improbable but very funny scenario involving the adult camp concept. The group then identified some Buyers and planned an information-gathering campaign and a Product comparison. In smaller groups, the writers sketched proposals for various treatments of the subject in several different media.

The Information Ozone is all around you. It's in the press, on computers, in libraries and bookstores, in surveys and polls and the Government Printing Office, and in a company newsletter. If you specialize in writing about a particular subject, you should be familiar with all the sources in your field. If you're a generalist, you should be casting a wider informational net.

You have to use your eyes and ears selectively in the Information Ozone and filter out a lot of useless garbage, but in some scrap of information there may be the germ of an idea, which could become a Product. If you're a fiction writer, the Information Ozone can help you cast your writing in a more commercial light, or even serve you more directly: One writer in my seminars reported using the bare outlines of life histories in obituary columns in creating fictional characters. Another writer who has sold "concepts" to television uses human-interest stories and features for script ideas. When he adapts personal stories for film, he must buy rights to the stories of the principal characters; in some cases, he outlines fictional treatments of the general subject.

An alert writer eavesdrops whenever and wherever possible. He never takes a plane or train trip without engaging his seatmate in conversation. He may occasionally be bored silly, but he may also glean an idea or piece of information that can be useful in creating a Product. He talks to strangers often, whenever it's appropriate and possible, and he's always aware of the commercial potential of what he hears or learns. And he's quick to spot the beginning of a trend and use it to create for carefully targeted Buyers.

Some writers not only spot trends but actually make them happen. Journalist Marie Brenner calls this "putting a gloss on any trend and shining it up to a life-style"; critics call it gross generalization. It's a preferred technique for life-style writers, who are in great demand in the consumer periodical press and, once they have been anointed by identification in that medium, are courted by book publishers.

The writers who spot and polish trends are soon identified by Buyers as experts, whether their specialty is this year's "in" psychological syndrome or this decade's new sexual option or this week's new favorite fad, style, or pursuit. They are not usually experts in the academic sense; their particular skill is in knowing when something is or has become important enough to a measurable population to interest a Buyer. They also know where to find and how to quote the real experts in the relevant field. Life-style writers can profit most from the Information Ozone, although every specialist should be in touch with and become a presence in the Information Ozone of his particular field because that's how he gets on the right mailing lists. A life-style writer, for example, is someone who reads a statistic about the number of first-time mothers over thirty and can think of five ways to use that information—in a book, a film, a play, an article, a series. In the nonfiction book market, life-style writers often have an edge over specialists, since their writing encompasses such a broad and usually economically attractive audience. These writers are skilled at generalizing from statistics, creating a style from sometimes isolated examples. Their slick magazine articles sometimes end up on movie screens, as *Saturday Night Fever* did and as will a recent *Rolling Stone* cover story on singles and health clubs.

EXPLOITING YOUR LIFE—MAYBE

As you search for a marketable idea, it's often useful to begin with the advice given by every creative writing teacher: Start with what you know, especially if what you know might be interesting to others. Begin with a subject or topic familiar and interesting to you and do enough basic research to identify a market of like-minded Customers. Mining your own life experience can be a good beginning. Many books, articles, and films began in writers' minds as attempts to clarify their personal histories or deal with their emotional aftermath. Writers skilled at transforming their experience movingly, cleverly, or dramatically often have little difficulty selling their work. Woody Allen may be the single exception to my rule that a writer should never waste on a psychiatrist material that could make a book!

A banal expression that irritated me every time I heard my advertising agency boss say it turned out to be the single most useful piece of advice I've ever taken. "If life hands you a lemon, make lemonade," he'd say, and my first book, *Sex and the Single Parent,* was the result. So are hundreds of other articles, plays, books, and films, from novels like *Fear of Flying* to nonfiction best-sellers such as *I'm Dancing as Fast as I Can.* If what has happened in your life can yield well-written truth, exploitation, or advice that could be interesting or useful to others, turn it into a Product. Sell what you know, if you can determine that others might profit from or be entertained or stimulated by it.

TEACHING YOUR TRADE OR HOBBY

If you teach or practice a trade, hobby, or profession, consider whether you can distill that knowledge into a salable book or article. The demand for some kinds of how-to and self-help books eased for a while but lately has begun to build again, especially in certain subject areas. Somewhere in the Information Ozone you can find the supporting data needed to convince a Buyer that a market exists for your specialty. And cultural diversity, a writer's best friend, has created identifiable markets for many books in the self-help category. As John Naisbitt says, self-help has always been part of American life. In Naisbitt's projection of trends that will transform our lives, this will not change. In fact, it will become even more important as people move from reliance on institutional help to self-reliance. Books will continue to play an important part in the self-help movement, as will magazines, which are increasingly service-oriented. And narrowcast marketing by publishers may mean that it is profitable to provide information to a specific population that can be reached by a carefully targeted marketing effort.

If you can put what you know into words and can identify a market for your information, you can do more than simply get published. You can also add luster to your professional reputation, get onto the lucrative lecture circuit, and experience the real pleasure of helping people help themselves.

FINDING A NEW ANGLE

Expertise in a subject counts but even more critical is a new way to feature it, especially if it is in one of the perennially in-demand areas such as how to get rich, how to get thin, or how to stay in love. A look at the best-seller lists indicates that the popularity of these topics has not waned in recent years. As an example, a writer in one of my seminars who counseled two-career couples in her therapy practice devised techniques to help her clients make the emotional and mental transition from their professional milieus to their personal lives. As soon as I saw her written proposal, based on her own practice, I knew it was marketable and that any trade publisher with an understanding of market demographics would agree. She titled her proposal *Leaving the Office Behind.* Her theme was topical, her knowledge easily transferrable to print, her writing imaginative and clear, and her market of potential Customers as big as the most recent statistic on the total number of two-career families (and their strong purchasing power). Her well-written proposal excited several Buyers and was sold to the highest bidder among them simply because she had identified and used a new angle on an old idea—how to improve a love relationship.

SELLING IT AS MANY TIMES IN AS MANY PLACES AS YOU CAN

The more a writer writes about a particular subject, the more frequently Buyers will seek him out to write again on that topic. Amortizing your research and information-collecting hours pays off when you can use the same basic material in a number of different formats and markets. If you specialize, your topic may be of more interest than you realize: as a column in a general magazine, as a chapter in a book, as part of a larger whole, rather than just in the markets that are obvious matches for your material. At current magazine rates, if you can't make your information do double, triple, or even greater duty, you're losing money.

WHAT WILL SELL AND IS IT MEANINGFUL?

At just about this point in my seminars, a writer raises his hand and asks a question that goes something like this: "How do you resolve the conflict between writing what you know they will buy and writing something really meaningful and important?" The implication that something of interest to more than ten people (that is, commercial) is somehow less than significant is not lost on me; it perfectly embodies the attitude of literary aesthetes and small-minded intellectuals. Every writer who depends on sales to survive makes his own choice on that issue. There are some topics that sell for which I could not muster up enough enthusiasm or concern to write even a proposal, no matter how certain the sale was. But, fortunately, there are plenty of good ideas that do turn me on, and I'm bound to write better about them. And when I—or you—run out of those, the Information Ozone is teeming with more.

NOW THAT YOU HAVE
A GREAT IDEA . . .

THE MEDIUM IS
THE MESSAGE

The Muse dropped by and found you in; the bank called to report that you're on MasterCard's Most Wanted List; you've mined the Information Ozone and come up with a golden nugget. From whatever source, you've come up with an idea and you can't get it out of your head. Still you're not sure what to do with it. A book? A movie? A magazine article? You must make a decision about the medium—the means of expression—before you put paper in the typewriter.

That decision may be predetermined by your own "writerly" leanings. Some talented writers are deft in all media, equally capable of turning out books, articles, scripts, and plays—William Goldman, author of dozens of screenplays, novels, and nonfiction books is one. But most writers are fluent—at the start of their careers anyway—in only one form, and if you are such a person, you will attempt to mold, shape, twist, or contort your idea into whatever form that happens to be.

While that may seem to make sense to you, it does not necessarily mean that your idea is as suited to your medium as the market is. Every idea is not appropriate for every form of expression; in fact, many publishers often reject proposals on the grounds that they are unsuitable for the book market, just as producers turn down good books and book ideas because they don't lend themselves to the requirements of filmmakers.

A writer who came to one of my seminars had spent months researching doctors with drug abuse problems and wanted to write a book about it. Several publishers had rejected his proposal. Said one, "If you had a solution to this problem we might be interested. Simply telling the scope of the problem is not enough; such a book would depress the reader." A medical textbook publisher also rejected the proposal because the writer was not a medical professional, adding, "Although we are aware that this problem does exist in the profession, we feel that it is sufficiently covered in medical ethics texts."

Magazine editors queried by this writer were no more enthusiastic, although one suggested that it might be publishable if the writer turned it into a service piece: "We might be interested in 'Ten Ways to Know If Your Doctor Is an Abuser, and What to Do If He Is,'" she said. And an agent, the last person approached by the writer, said, "Nobody wants to spend twenty dollars on a 'downer'—a book with questions but no solutions to something over which most people have little or no control."

The writer was stubborn and would not give up. Eventually he found a television producer who was interested enough to option the rewritten proposal, now a television outline that told the story of a marriage and career nearly destroyed by drugs. The writer had put his information in the appropriate format, retitled it dramatically, and described it in his cover letter to the producer in a brief phrase that could have been a *TV Guide* listing: "Young doctor under stress writes own prescriptions for trouble but is saved from self-destruction by faith, strength, and support from his kindly mentor." What clinched the sale was the authenticity provided by the real-life subject of the story; the writer had secured the rights to the doctor's life story for a one-dollar option before submitting the outline to producers. This writer had no experience in television writing. He had studied the format, however, and written a proposal that was strong enough to interest a Buyer. He may not get to write the television script; chances are that the Buyer will bring in a more experienced, "bankable" writer for the film. But this writer has made some money, has the promise of more if the option is exercised, and has a Buyer who may solicit more ideas from him. He may not have a talent for writing films, but the money will subsidize him until he comes up with another idea he can turn into a book.

Perhaps you've never considered adapting that novel you've been working on into a film treatment, or turning that short story into a magazine article. But if you're beginning to think like a selling writer, you'll start asking yourself, "How can I use this?"

Here's another example from my seminars: A writer had been trying to sell her novel about a young dancer without success, although she had spent two years researching the making of a ballerina. She put some of that information into a proposal geared toward a magazine for parents, titled it "If Your Daughter Wants to Be a Dancer," and received four positive responses to her query letter. Another writer reworked a rejected article proposal about crib death and found several potential Buyers among television producers. Still another revised an outline for a film about drug dealing and turned it into the first four chapters of a novel.

If the idea has grabbed you by the throat and will not let go, you'll find a Buyer for it; it just may not be the one you originally had in mind. Generally speaking, the strength of the idea, its topicality, and its suitability to the medium can sell a project to periodicals and films; in the book market, the quality of the writing is at least as important as the commercial potential of the idea.

THE UNTOUCHABLE IDEA AND THE DOWNER TOPIC

There are ideas that some Buyers said they would never touch (and are making handsome profits on today), others that they cannot touch, and a few that they will not touch. But those distinctions are blurring as the nation's demographics change: Says a publisher, *"No More Hot Flashes and Other Good News* is a book no one would have bought ten years ago. But everyone's getting older, and people aren't just accepting the limitations and infirmities of middle or old age the way they used to." The distinctions between the untouchable and the acceptable subjects are also blurring as previously taboo topics like rape, incest, and child abuse are addressed more frequently in the daily news. Nuclear war is making money in print and film these days—the unthinkable is suddenly frighteningly thinkable. Cancer is another subject generating more book ink today—more families are touched by it, and more publishers are servicing them with books on the topic.

Still, dealing with a Downer topic is chancy for a writer. The most reliable way to sell a Downer is to have a solution for it, whether the subject is death, old age, violence, poverty, or fat. Or to have such a lucid and brilliant explanation for or explication of it that it will appeal to a Buyer's aesthetic sensibility. (Yes, publishers, editors, and filmmakers do have such a sensibility. It's just that commerce so often gets in its way.)

There is another way to sell a Downer, which is to self-publish it and put your information directly into the hands of the appropriate Customers, but I'll come to that later. The point is that an idea cannot be considered out of context. It has to be matched to the right Buyer, and that Buyer may be in a medium in which you are not fluent or which you have no interest in pursuing or of which you lack knowledge. Do not let that stop you. If the idea is good enough and if you are a skillful enough writer, you can learn the form.

TIMING THE IDEA

Some good ideas never get out of a writer's head and onto paper or film; at least, not by their own efforts. The ideas linger in an unused corner of the cerebellum until someone else turns them into articles, books, or movies. Or until they've been filmed, written, and discussed so much that no one is interested anymore. Topicality is extremely important to periodicals, relatively important to film-makers (especially television), and moderately important to book publishers. And all of these Buyers think ahead, so you must, too. Three months before the Olympic Games is too late to propose an illustrated history of the Olympics to a publisher, and April is too late to sell a Mother's Day essay to a magazine. Magazines have lead times of six weeks to six months, depending on their frequency of publication. The usual amount of time between acceptance of a finished manuscript and completion of a sale-ready book is nine to twelve months. The minimum time needed to complete a television film after acceptance of the final script is six months. And the post-production time for a typical theatrical film is at least a year. You must be aware of these publishing cycles in order to ensure that your idea is timely as well as interesting, commercial, and well written.

Some ideas are old two minutes after the ink is dry in the book or magazine that printed them, and others endure regardless of how many times, in how many ways, they are explored and explained. Judging how long a trend will last or when it will peak keeps editors and publishers and filmmakers reaching for their ulcer medication; so does knowing that exact point at which the market is oversaturated. Knowing when ideas will find the most fertile climate for acceptance is a talent the selling writer must cultivate, and the Information Ozone is a place to start.

SPECIALIST OR GENERALIST?

The two decisions writers usually make at the beginning of their careers relate to the medium in which they write and the subject matter with which they ordinarily deal. Those decisions are typically based on talent and inclination, and they should be based on marketability. A good writer can adapt his skills to the best medium for his idea; a flexible writer can widen the narrow area of his expertise and create more selling opportunities as he does.

Whether you write for the periodical or the book trade, some degree of specialization can help you build a reputation with Buyers. After a few articles or a book on one subject, in the minds of your Buyers you may become, by default or intent, an Expert. Because of this reputation, you may be the writer who is considered when a Buyer needs or wants a book in your particular area. But you may also be pigeonholed as a one-subject writer, and if that subject has no current appeal, you'll be out of luck.

If you are or have been a specialist and find publishing opportunities in your field dwindling, it may be time to consider how you can use your particular expertise as a stepping-stone to a wider market. If you are at the beginning of your career and plan to specialize in writing on one topic or in one medium, take the following into account:

• Can your subject hold your interest for a long time?

- Will it interest a growing number of people in the foreseeable future—long enough to make it pay for you to become an Expert?
- Are there too many other well-known writers in your area, who sell regularly to your Buyers?
- Does the subject lend itself to expansion into other tangential or larger categories?

A writer who began by publishing a local shopping guide decided that she was interested in food, and had a regional cookbook published. In the course of researching food, she discovered that she was really more interested in wine. She set out to make herself a wine writer, at a time when her area of the country was beginning to develop a major wine industry; there were no national writers covering this area, so she began to get assignments from national wine, food, and entertainment periodicals. She then sold a handful of travel pieces with wine-country touring angles. Restaurant reviews and some regional lifestyle pieces followed, and when wine growers invited her to visit their vineyards in other parts of the world, she expanded her market as a travel writer. As her expertise increased, so did her interests and her markets; as she exhausted the possibilities in one relatively narrow area, more opened up in allied fields. She now supplements her salary as an executive in the wine industry with regular freelance book and magazine assignments in food, wine, travel, and shelter publications and at this writing has two regionally and one nationally published books to her credit.

An idea, well-executed, becomes a Product; a Product either dead-ends in terms of future Products or opens up more sales in different markets. A writer should consider every idea in this context. Beyond the intrinsic rewards—artistic, professional, and financial—of turning this idea into a Product is this question: What (or who) will this lead to? No selling writer should expect to earn enough money to retire on any one Product, and even if most of your attention is focused on the Product you're developing or selling right now, the next should not be far from your thoughts. And your current Product should be one that will generate additional ones with other markets, different media, more buyer contacts, and new opportunities.

KEEPING THE IDEAS COMING

Your professional energies should be divided among the following: completing your current Product and meeting your deadlines; redefining and refining other ideas and turning them into Products; selling your existing inventory of unsold Products (manuscripts and revised proposals) to new Buyers. With what's left of your time (although this is especially difficult for a writer with a full-time job) you should be reading, reading, and reading, as well as making contact with your industry and keeping an eye on what's going on at the point of sale.

Does this seem like a great deal of work? It is. Being a writer is being an entrepreneur, and that means keeping enough Products selling to make an impact on the market and on your wallet, and enough ideas coming to generate new Products.

When an idea becomes a Product and then turns into a contract with a deadline, you'll have less time to devote to other Products. But you cannot afford to neglect that part of your business. You should keep three sets of files and allocate your daily work hours among current, pending, and future Products. "Current" represents material sold and in the process of completion; "pending" includes proposals circulating among Buyers for sale; "future" is an immense file of ideas that are waiting to be turned into Products.

One good idea can launch your career as a writer. But one good idea is never enough.

IDENTIFYING YOUR BUYERS: THE MAGAZINE PRESS

Since the narrowcasting has taken over magazine marketing, matching your idea to the Customer is of primary importance when you sell to the periodical press. When you can identify your Customer, you'll know where to look for the Buyer; he's publishing the magazine that Customer reads. But if you don't develop your idea in a way that speaks directly to his Customer, you'll turn off that Buyer before he's even read your fabulous prose. Magazine editors complain constantly that writers never seem to have read their magazine before trying to sell to it. You may have written the world's best study of menopause, for example, but if you send it to *Cosmopolitan* they won't even read past the first sentence; their readers are not your Customers. An article that works for a magazine aimed at one particular Customer can occasionally be reworked for another, but if your magazine proposals are rejected more often than they are purchased, you may not have a sharp enough image of the Customer to identify your Buyer's needs.

One good way to learn a great deal about the precise target audience of a specific magazine is to study the material prepared by its advertising department to help clients decide whether or not to advertise in the magazine. Among these materials is a profile of the typical reader by age, education, income, interests, and so on. You can get a reader profile by writing to the appropriate department of the magazine and implying that you have a product or service you might advertise in the magazine, and, in a way, that's true. Or you could ask someone you know in an ad agency to procure whatever sales or research material the magazine provides for its ad clients. Use your ingenuity and find a way to put your hands on that information; it is the best guide to the Customer the Buyer wants to reach.

Even without a reader profile, there are plenty of clues to tell you who your Customer is and how to shape your idea into a Product that will meet his needs as well as your Buyer's. Study the table of contents of each issue carefully; see which departments within the magazine seem to be related to your idea and who edits those sections. Watch the way the magazine advertises itself to advertisers in its ads in newspapers such as the *New York Times* and in the advertising industry trade press—*Advertising Age,* for instance. Once you've found a magazine that seems right for your Product, read at least the last two years of issues; there are only so many subjects of interest to each group of Customers, and yours may already have been covered by the magazine (though that should not dissuade you if you have an entirely new slant on the subject). Research the editorial requirements of the magazine in a publishing-trade book like *Writer's Market.* And read the editor's column in the magazine, which may report on its own surveys of readers.

If you've done all these things and still can't seem to get a fix on the Customer, it may be that the magazine is changing its editorial focus—not unusual today, when every magazine publisher is trying to narrowcast tightly enough to attract and hold an identifiable share of the market. Such mixed messages may indicate that there has been a decision to modify the magazine's editorial content to reflect changes in that market. Clues to shifts in editorial emphasis will also be reported, in most cases, in the magazine industry press.

Last year, for example, *Redbook* changed ownership and management and then marketing strategy. It redefined its target audience, a move announced in a series of national newspaper and advertising trade publications in which *Redbook* was proclaimed "the magazine for the juggler"—the woman who juggles home and career. Thus a piece about a housewife in the suburbs with no job outside her home might not be as appealing to the magazine today as it might have been a few years ago, when the suburban woman was its Customer.

Never assume that because a publication had a particular readership some time ago it is still courting the same audience. Over the years magazines have been engaged in a life-and-death struggle for a market saturated by competing media; those that have survived and those newly created hold closely to their target audience and keep up with that audience as it changes interests, priorities, and life-styles. As new interests and markets evolve, new magazines spring up to serve them; even new products, like personal computers, have spawned new magazines. As the median age of the population changes, as the baby-boom generation moves into full-scale consumerism, and as the information age takes hold, the magazine market is changing too. Read *Magazine Industry Market Place* and similar reference books for an up-to-date list of publications, and spend as much time as you can in a good magazine store.

Until you know exactly who the Customer is for a particular publication, don't even start writing your proposal. For writers who can deliver what magazine Buyers want today, the possibilities are very good. But to take advantage of them you must be flexible; you must be able to change and shape an idea like clay, until you have molded it into *exactly* what the Buyer wants. And after you've sold to that magazine, you must shape and change your idea again for the next Buyer.

Here are the questions you should ask and answer about a proposed magazine piece before you start to frame the proposal:

- How many buyers are there for this information and material?
- Can this idea be adapted to both general and specialty magazines?
- How many times can you sell your idea?
- How many Products can you make out of it?
- How many articles must you sell to amortize the cost of research?
- Can you sell to at least one Buyer in each of the three magazine classifications—general-interest, consumer, and trade, technical, or professional journals?
- Can you sell your material twice (in different versions, of course) to two different Buyers in any or all of those groups?

A travel writer from one of my seminars spent three weeks in Europe. When she came to the seminar, she had sold one newspaper article about her trip and one travel piece. After the seminar she used what she'd learned and slanted her material to several other audiences. She produced these proposals: "Retiring in the Greek Islands," for a magazine aimed at senior citizens; "A Woman's Guide to Meeting Those Marvelous Mediterranean Men," for a magazine with an age 18 to 25 target audience; "Everything You Always Wanted to Know About Flokati Rugs," for a shelter magazine; "Greece's American First Lady," for a feminist journal.

Another writer, a newspaper reporter, used his series of articles on a notorious local criminal for pieces in three different magazines: a true crime/detective magazine, a woman's magazine, and a weekly news magazine. Ultimately all of these proposals resulted in a contract for a nonfiction book and an option for a television movie.

Do not be afraid of trying to open up new magazine markets for your work. Be willing to adapt your material to as many different outlets in as many different ways as you can.

What makes a writer able to move nimbly from market to market is not just identifying the Customer and, through him, the Buyer, but being able to project himself into the magazine Customer's identity. This is an acting exercise that will serve you well; after all, a writer's creativity comes from more than just being good with words. As you begin to consider a new market, ask yourself what you know or can learn about its Customers— how they live and think and spend and work and worship and play. Put your idea into your imaginary Customer's mind. What is it about your information that will serve, interest, or entertain him? Why should he care to know what you have to say? What are the benefits for him in reading your work? The answers to these questions turn an idea into a Product.

Here is a final example, from my own "pending" file, of how to turn one idea into several Products. Recently I received a new foundation report on corporate approaches to day care and wrote one proposal based on it that was slanted toward working mothers (a market identified by a magazine with that exact readership, for which I regularly write). I aimed another proposal at a magazine for executive women, whose editor is also a regular Buyer of mine. Those were the most obvious Buyers. Others who might be interested include a professional management journal, since the quality of information in the report would appeal to the business community; a city magazine appropriate to the area studied in the report; a banking magazine, since the report indicated that several banks have achieved limited employee turnover by subsidizing day care for employees' children; and a journal of human behavior, which would be interested in what the report said about the emotional adjustment of children to on-site day care.

RESELLING YOUR WORK AND THE ECONOMICS OF SYNDICATION

When you sell the same material (used differently, of course) to several Buyers, it's important to clarify contractually just what rights each Buyer has purchased. If you are a full-time journalist, you should check with your employer about his policy on reselling material collected while in his employ or used in his publication. If you are a freelance writer, you should sell only first serial or first North American rights to your articles (for further information, see page 135). That way, if another publication wants to reprint or syndicate your work, you must be repaid for it. Some newspapers, such as the *New York Times* and the *Washington Post,* often syndicate material to their groups of papers in other parts of the country. And some syndicates occasionally buy work by freelance or staff writers for use in a number of their client papers.

A word about syndication: Many writers want to sell syndicated columns. What few understand is that the economics of syndication make it all but impossible for writers to earn much money unless they are syndicated in hundreds of newspapers several times a week, like Ann Landers or other feature columnists. Most newspapers can buy even the most popular syndicated columns for less than ten dollars apiece, and ordinarily only half of that money goes to the writer—the rest goes to the syndicate. So one would have to be syndicated in at least a hundred outlets to earn what the average magazine might pay for first-time rights to the work. If you are still interested in tackling the syndicate market, the items necessary in making a sale are similar to those needed for selling to a magazine or book Buyer: several sample columns, a proposal with good market data and supporting facts and figures, and a strong reason-to-buy aimed at the syndicate editor, whose name and other particulars you will find in *LMP*.

7

IDENTIFYING YOUR BUYERS: THE BOOK TRADE

Matching your idea to the market is easier to do with magazines than it is with books. While in periodicals you identify the Buyer by focusing on the Customer, in books you look for a Buyer who is already servicing a large number of potential Customers and offer him a Product that will appeal to a segment rather than to the total of all those Customers, just as he balances his list by providing so much fiction, so much nonfiction, so many craft, hobby, or self-help titles, etc.

If a glance at a Buyer's catalog indicates that he never publishes the kind of material you've written, it would be pointless to try to sell your Product to him. Even though some large trade houses may seem to be attempting to be all things to all Customers, under various lines or imprints, this is not necessarily the case. Some, for instance, never publish very literary fiction, a few do not offer many business titles, others have no line of craft, hobby, or cookbooks, others don't issue mystery novels or westerns. If a Buyer's catalog indicates that he does, on occasion, publish books similar to yours, even if it's only one or two titles each list, you may want to consider him. But trying to educate a Buyer to change his marketing mix to include something quite untypical of his house is a waste of time.

Each trade house does have a personality and is most comfortable publishing the kind of book that has been successful for it in the past. As an article in a recent *Authors Guild Bulletin* points out, "It is patently wasteful to send a proposal on a cosmetics book for working women to Basic Books, or a manuscript on the virtues of astrology to Freeman or *Scientific American,* and yet authors do this kind of thing all the time."

Because the big trade houses publish the largest number of titles, most book writers approach them first, particularly fiction writers. But book publishers are beginning to narrowcast like magazines do, and finding the most compatible home for your Product is not impossible, even though the match you seek probably will not be as precise as it must be in periodicals.

You begin your search for the right Buyer for your book by shopping the market; by noting the publishers who've already indicated their interest in your subject by offering books about it; by checking the *Subject Guide to Books in Print,* found in all libraries and most bookstores; by further checking bookstore and library shelves. This is standard data collection for nonfiction writers, but you can and should do a similar kind of market survey if you write fiction too. You check the books most like your own in style, quality, and type, and find out who their publishers are. If you are writing genre or category fiction, find the publisher who has already developed an imprint for science fiction, romances, mysteries, westerns, or male adventures. For other kinds of novels, determine through publishers' catalogs (listed in *Publishers' Trade List Annual,* or available by request from publishers themselves) which houses devote a major portion of their lists to fiction, especially new fiction. While the trade houses are all in the blockbuster novel sweepstakes, some have a greater commitment to midlist or experimental fiction than others. In order to sell a novel to one of the big trade houses—Putnam's, William Morrow, Simon & Schuster, for instance—you must already be a writer of blockbusters, or be anyone at all who has a novel with enough commercial appeal to generate subsidiary rights sales to book clubs and paperback houses or whose writing quality is so extraordinary that sales may be forthcoming after the reviewers have agreed that it is, indeed, Art.

There is much discussion in the industry about the fact that so-called midlist fiction is losing ground to blockbusters and that the money required to purchase the latter dries up funding resources for the former. Publishers deny this and point to the number of first novels they publish each list—a piddling percentage by anyone's standards except their own. Midlist hardcover fiction is neither experimental nor inherently commercial. This group of novels sells between 7500 and 20,000 copies each, is not category fiction, and doesn't set the world on fire. It's not a big winner in terms of sales, but it's not usually a big loser, either. Calling a book midlist fiction is like saying a girl has a nice personality.

Midlist fiction is not beloved by trade publishers. The economics of publishing leave little leeway for putting out a Product that will not earn back its investment, let alone return a profit. Each house calculates the direct and indirect costs of publishing a book before purchasing it from a writer, and the method of calculation is different from house to house. In every one, however, each book is treated as a profit center, and each must justify its purchase. Thus the total amount of money available for purchasing fiction, whatever that dollar figure, is less meaningful than the money available to purchase each book, which is determined after the probable economics are worked out, based on how much the book will cost to produce; what other costs are involved, including advertising and distribution; how much revenue can be earned from the book's sale; and how quickly its costs can be recovered.

It is important for writers to consider very basic publishing economics, particularly if their books would be costly to produce or are not obviously commercial or of significant enough literary quality to promise a decent return on investment. Because that is what determines whether a big trade house, especially one owned by a conglomerate, will buy noncategory fiction.

If your fiction falls in the midlist category, don't give up. Much work of this type sells to mass market paperback publishers, who originate as well as reprint books. More and more new fiction of varying literary, commercial, or exploitative merit is published this way, and it's just a matter of identifying those Buyers.

For fiction and nonfiction writers, the big trade publishers seem to offer the greatest potential for sales. But, in fact, this is not necessarily true. According to Bowker's Data Services, in 1983 there were more than 15,000 active publishers who are responsible for over 619,000 titles in print. But only three percent of those publishers account for eighty percent of the titles, "still leaving more than 100,000 titles accounted for by about 14,000 presumably smaller publishers," as *Publishers Weekly* says. And some of the smaller ones may do a better job of publishing, promoting, and selling your product than one of the Big Few. The smaller publishers may offer a novice writer a much less competitive environment; in the Majors, many are seen but few are chosen, and those few are most likely to be selected from writers with good prior publishing credits or books that show great promise when Buyers do the numbers.

There are several alternatives to selling to a big trade publisher. These include small presses, subsidy publishers, book packagers, and the process of self-publishing.

DEFINING AND FINDING THE RIGHT
SMALL PRESS

There are hundreds of small or independent publishers that are often overlooked by writers of fiction and nonfiction, and for one good reason: lack of up-front money, the advance that feeds and sustains you during those long months of writing and wrestling with the Muse. The independent publishers rarely have the wherewithal to make more than a token advance payment. But there are other rewards that for some writers may be reason enough to publish with an independent.

A client whose first book was sold to an independent and whose next was purchased by a trade publisher for a very small advance described the difference: "At the first house I felt involved in a partnership, as if both the publisher and I were trying to do the same thing—publish the best book we could, from design to typesetting and, of course, writing, and try to keep it in print as long as possible while trying to reach our own special audience, people who read good short fiction. My second book simply got lost at the trade house. It got less promotional attention than any of the fifty books on that list, and there was no effort to keep it alive long enough for its own natural customers to find it. I felt like a commodity there, and didn't make very much more money to boot."

Over the long run, in fact, that writer made more money with the independent, which had paid her an advance of less than a thousand dollars but sold the book over a four-year period. The two-thousand-dollar advance she received from the trade publisher was all the money she *ever* received from it. Her first book is still in print and she earns a few hundred dollars annually from its sales.

Many small presses offer the writer of serious fiction and/or poetry a much happier publishing experience than big houses can. And over time the title may sell more copies if independently published than if done with a trade publisher. There are small presses whose most successful books have been distributed by trade houses or sold to mass market reprinters. Even without that result, some books published by small presses have achieved maximum market penetration, including in the chain bookstores or with big book wholesalers.

Big publishers demand that a book show a quick return on investment, and the rate of return may be more important than the amount. So the house's maximum expenditures of time and money on any list go to the books that promise the quickest and biggest return on investment—the sure things, the blockbusters, the works of an established author with a proven sales record. All of this means that your book must have something more going for it than its intrinsic quality and readability. That quality must be validated by superb reviews, big subsidiary rights sales, and the unbridled enthusiasm of the publisher, senior editor, and sales manager, or it's never going to get from your Buyer to your Customer. It may even be returned, unopened, ninety days after publication, never having seen the light of a bookstore window.

Small presses want to be profitable, too, but their reasons for publishing are often not just economic ones. Many independents specialize in a style or type of book that meets a literary, political, social, or aesthetic need for the house. If your book can fill one or more of these needs, you will find a Buyer among the independents. Some of those publishers don't expect to get rich, so you shouldn't either, but that doesn't mean their standards for books carrying their name are lower than those of the big trade publishers. In many cases, the small houses are choosier than the big ones because they risk their available capital on a much smaller list of titles and every one must show some return, or at least pay for itself if they are to stay in business. Small presses can and do specialize in narrow categories, which represent only a portion of the Product mix a trade house offers its Customers. Many independents grew out of one-shot books or Products that caught on. These houses increase their number of titles very slowly; they try not to grow so fast that they can't devote a meaningful allocation of time and money to each one. So if you have just written the outline for, say, *How to Keep Your DeLorean Alive,* you might look into John Muir Publications, which has sold over two million copies of books offering similar advice to the owners of Volkswagens and Hondas. Or try your proposal for your manuscript of *The Cliterati: Secret Lives of Women Writers* at the Feminist Press, whose name is self-explanatory. Or send Ten Speed Press your outline for *Getting Fired: Surviving a Hole in Your Parachute.*

Now are you getting the idea? There is a match for your product out there somewhere, and if you write for an audience that an independent has identified—an audience of a particular social, political, aesthetic, even sexual or ethnic homogeneity—you'll find it. There may be categories of this type within a particular trade house, but often it's easier to compete in the independent market.

Among existing publishers, there are small presses and minuscule ones and some that are hardly distinguishable from trade houses. Ten Speed, for example, publishes only ten titles a year, but its average press run is 25,000, larger than some of the Majors. Scarecrow Press's typical run per title is 1000 copies, but it brings out over one hundred books a year. Some independents will pay you in books, which you can then sell yourself; others will offer tiny advances; most will pay standard author royalties of ten to fifteen percent; and almost every one will give your book more individual attention throughout the editorial, production, and marketing phases of publishing than a Major will, unless the Major has earmarked it for the Big Treatment—huge advertising budget, big promotional tour, the works.

You may not get rich with a small press, but there's no guarantee that you'll achieve that goal with a trade house, either. What is certain is that if you publish with a small press, even one tied into its own distribution network, you'll have to help your Buyer sell his Customer if you are ever to realize any return at all on your investment. You're going to have to be creative in marketing your Product directly to the Customer, a task that some writers may find even more distasteful than having to deal with a Buyer (after all, you can do most of that by correspondence). Small presses usually have no budget for advertising and no personnel devoted solely to publicity. So these tasks may fall to you, or to someone you hire, like a publicist. Marketing yourself can be a very expensive proposition and a time-consuming one, so in choosing a smaller Buyer consider whether you're willing or able to do it.

As small presses command an increasingly larger share of the book market, they are also narrowcasting and trying to serve their identifiable and disparate groups of readers rather than compete for a share of the Customers in a random general market. If your Product can be targeted to those populations that traditionally purchase the titles of small presses, it may ultimately reward you more to look among them for a Buyer. While studies indicate that there is relatively little brand loyalty among the Major publishers—people don't buy books by publisher, they purchase them by title or author—this is not always true with the independents, which often court the small retail outlets catering to their particular market.

Remember: Three percent of all publishers account for eighty percent of the published books, and the competition to get your Product bought by one of the Majors is very, very tough; the economic test it must meet as well as those of commercial or artistic merit increase such competition. But there are 14,000 other Buyers out there surviving in the marketplace, and among them they publish over

100,000 books. To consider only the big trade houses that comprise the fortunate three percent as your potential Buyers is to eliminate an enormous chunk of your market. Among the smaller presses are religious publishers, university presses, textbook publishers, playbook publishers . . . a Buyer for every decently written Product.

THE RIGHT BOOKS TO SELF-PUBLISH

When there is a specific market that is absolutely in need of your book and you know how to reach that market easily and economically, manufacturing and distributing your Product can be highly profitable. A psychologist who came to my seminar had a unique, workable therapy method for a specific problem, which could be learned and reinforced with workbooks and tapes. He had a built-in market among his own client list for them and for the book he wanted to write. Every time he gave a lecture, conducted a workshop, or spoke at a conference he interfaced with potential Customers. His extensive list of former clients was the nucleus of a 1500-copy initial printing, and referrals from former clients accounted for another few hundred annually. In time, he might interest a trade publisher as his reputation grew and he had greater sales; for now, however, he could sell his self-published book strictly through his own resources and pocket eight dollars on each copy of a book that cost him only two dollars a copy. Another client self-published a highly specialized manual on dental instrumentation and sold over 6000 copies of it with the help of a mailing list from the company that manufactured the instrument. Her profit, after production costs, was over six dollars per book.

Both of these people wanted to publish with trade houses—for prestige, money, and the relief of having someone else take over the production and sale of their books, and, they thought, for access to a market larger than their own efforts could provide. The psychologist's desire was realistic; his easy-to-reach, pretested methods had appeal to a larger general market. The second writer was in a different position; the number of Customers with a real need to know what her very specialized book could tell them would not increase at all in that general market and could not be reached by a trade publisher any more economically, efficiently, or in greater numbers than she could do herself. If a publisher sold 6000 copies of her book at $7.95, she would realize less than a dollar a book.

When you can put your Product directly in the hands of Customers who need it, either by selling it yourself or through a professional in another field, you should self-publish it. That is particularly true when it is the kind of book that generally finds its way into a Customer's hands outside of normal bookselling channels. One writer in a recent seminar had tried, unsuccessfully, to market a book on funeral options to a trade house. When she applied the Theory of Looking Backward and considered the point of sale, she realized that few people react to the unexpected or even anticipated death of a loved one by dropping into a bookstore and buying a book on how to deal with death's aftermath. By putting herself in the Customer's place, she could project a scenario in which some professional—a clergyman, coroner, hospital administrator, even a funeral home director—would be able to place her Product in the hands of the Customer whose needs and problems it solved. And she could reach those people herself without a publisher's help.

Self-published books with good track records in the general market often attract the attention of large trade publishers. Peter McWilliams' computer books began that way, as did many other titles. Self-publishing requires an entirely different set of skills in addition to writing and selling. It also requires your own investment of money, unlike publishing with the trade houses or independents. But if you are prepared to function as your own producer and marketer as well as the writer, have a sound business plan for your Product, and can raise the money or fund it from other writing projects that Buyers pay you for, do not dismiss it out of hand.

In many cases, a self-published book can earn more money for its writer than the same book published by a trade house; the difference is that it's your money as well as your time that are at risk. You may be able to produce and market that book profitably while a trade house could not. If you determine that self-publishing holds potential for you, learn everything you can about the process from the Information Ozone. Begin by reading books that describe how self-publishing works, and talk to as many people as you can find who have self-published themselves. Go to conferences where experts in the field are available for consultation. Make yourself an expert even before you undertake the process. Decide whether you have the temperament, capital, and hustle to self-publish and if your Product is suitable.

SUBSIDY, SPONSORED, AND VANITY PUBLISHING

Subsidy or sponsored publishing and vanity publishing are often considered to be the same. In fact, there are important differences between them. According to the *Writer's Encyclopedia,* "Books that are financed by a company, association, institution, foundation, or other group to serve its interest in some direct or indirect way, written by either a freelance writer, an expert in a particular field, or a company employee" are subsidy or sponsored books. The writing fee varies, as do the details of who owns what after publication. Some sponsors will pay an author's fee as well as production costs, then distribute the books and pay no per-copy royalty, especially if they use the book as a premium or corporate image-builder. Sometimes a royalty is offered, on a different scale from that usually paid by trade publishers. Often a sponsor will add an extra thousand copies of the book to the initial print run and allow the writer to sell those books himself and keep all the proceeds.

If you've finally finished fine-tuning your manuscript *Fifty Ways to Use Your Food Processor When You Just Can't Eat Another Thing,* you might find a buyer in a company like Cuisinart (which might in turn make a distribution deal with the trade house that turned it down when you submitted the same proposal to their senior editor). If you're dying to write the corporate history of the Amalgamated Blunderbuss Company and Mr. Blunderbuss wants it in lieu of a dividend for his stockholders, he'll probably be glad to subsidize your research. If the Alumni Office of Rah Rah University could use your memoirs as a development tool, they'll probably be delighted to sponsor you. Occasionally, sponsored or subsidized books get beyond their original audience and make it onto a best-seller list, usually when the sponsor has made a distribution deal with a major house; the history of the Amway Corporation, which held its place on the *New York Times* best-seller list for months, is a good example.

Of course, he who pays the piper calls the tune, and out-and-out patronage, which is how some writers view sponsored or subsidy books, is often seen as having negative moral or ethical aspects. But if the issues raised by your particular piper or the control he exerts don't bother you or your principles, this kind of publishing option bears consideration.

Subsidy publishing means different things to different people. Many book people think of subsidy publishing as being the same as vanity publishing, but there is an important distinction that is not always made. Subsidy publishers are those sponsors who underwrite part or all of the cost of manufacturing and marketing your Product, while vanity presses require the author to foot the bill for the entire project, from typesetting to postage. To me, vanity presses are like slugs; they may have their place in the evolutionary chain, but that's simply not sufficient reason for them to exist.

Vanity presses can be distinguished by their ads, those all-type oblongs that occasionally appear in the editorial section of your newspaper near or on the book page. In boldface type they proclaim, "Publisher looking for authors with Manuscripts!" Vantage is the best known of these companies, though there are others. The disadvantages of doing business with a vanity press range from never having the books reviewed (critics ignore offerings from vanity presses) to rarely having them distributed. What a vanity press does do is charge you a stiff fee to publish your book, a fee you can eliminate by self-publishing it if what you really want is a hardcover book with your name on it that will interest a very small number of people simply because you wrote it.

The primary reason vanity presses exist is apparent in their very name—vanity. I'm not making judgments on this—the desire to see your words in print is strong, and, if all else fails, you may wish to resort to getting there via this route. Vanity is necessary to the profession and is a great motivator for writers, although they call it ego rather than by its right name. But when a book has no other rationale for its existence, vanity is not always enough justification for a trade publisher to risk his money. A client in a recent seminar typified the usual easy prey of vanity presses. "My grandkids keep saying I should publish my memoirs of what it was like growing up on the farm in Montana at the turn of the century," she said. So far so good, except that her writing was simply not worthy of publication and there was nothing particularly unique about her story. She wanted, she said, to leave her family a published souvenir, and she was considering making a deal with a vanity press. Yet when she worked out the figures, she realized that she could have such a book self-published and avoid the markup charged by the vanity house for paper, printing, and binding (as well as the cost of their overhead and contributions to their retirement funds). Almost none of the fee charged by a vanity press goes to advertise, promote, or distribute the book, as promised in their glossy come-on brochures. And libraries as well as booksellers and critics avoid vanity books like the plague. So should you. There is nothing wrong with vanity as long as you don't pay more for it than it's worth.

BOOK PACKAGERS

When you're going through the process of identifying the Buyer who's absolutely right for your book Product, you may begin to hear the term "package" bandied about and wonder if it's an option you should consider. Usually packagers are "idea" people who look for writers to turn those ideas into Products. A packager functions like a publisher, except that he doesn't usually market or distribute the book; rather, he licenses a publisher to execute and sell the Product for him. Most books purchased by publishers from packagers are prepared and edited by the packager rather than the publisher. Packagers provide all editorial functions up to and occasionally including actual production of books and delivery to the publisher's warehouse. Some packagers rival publishers in scope of titles; Book Creations Incorporated, which packages series of paperback fiction and single volumes, has produced 234 titles, including the Wagons West series and the Windhaven series. Nor are packaged books distinguishable from any others that occasionally do bestselling business. *Items from Our Catalog,* a packaged trade paperback from Cloverdale Press which was licensed to Avon for distribution, has 800,000 copies in print.

Some packagers pay writers flat fees and others offer a portion of the royalties they earn from publishers. Many packagers leave it up to the publishers to whom they license their Products to do the actual selling; others are particularly good at getting their books into nontraditional retail outlets. One of the best reasons to go with a book packager is that when your Product is an idea or a concept that requires creative editing and equally creative illustrating and marketing, with follow-through not always available in trade publishing houses.

One question that often arises between writers and packagers is who owns what—whether the author, in working for a flat fee or for hire, forfeits any rights to other financial remuneration, such as royalties or percentages of subsidiary rights sales. Such details should be worked out carefully in advance, preferably with the assistant of an agent or lawyer. Think of packagers as middlemen between you and a publisher; if you need their skills, their clout, and their reputation to sell a book to a publisher and their marketing know-how to move it into the hands of the Customer, consider the packaging option. Make your skills and talents known to as many packagers as you can, all of whom are looking for commercial ideas and people to develop them under their guidance and direction.

Make sure the terms of your contract are fair. Understand what you're getting into—that's true of all publishing ventures, but especially so with packagers. And realize that small imprints within large trade houses often function in the same way that packagers do. In fact, they are in-house packagers, small operations designed to create and develop certain kinds of Products to be offered with the house's entire Product mix. Book packagers are outside the publishing houses, and when the trades buy from them, they are laying off some of their own risk. Consequently, the packager assumes much of the writer's risk and compensates him accordingly. Books such as *The Joy of Sex* and the *Handbook of Separation Techniques for Chemical Engineers* began as packages; that should give you some idea of the range of possibilities in packaging for you, the writer.

Some books are particularly suited to packagers, especially those that require expensive illustration or time-consuming editorial efforts, like encyclopedias or other reference books or collections. If you've written *The Illustrated Guide to Cheap Motels* or *The Whole Ice Cream Catalog,* a packager may be for you. Most packagers started at large trade houses as editors but saw the need for a separate operation to create, produce, and maintain control over the execution of certain books that could then be offered to other publishers who could market them efficiently. As a sort of boutique editorial and production department whose overhead and errors they do not have to cover, the packager is sometimes exceedingly attractive to a trade house—more so than you, alone out there with your idea, which requires expensive and extensive help to develop into a profitable Product.

What a packager is to you, the writer, is another Buyer, and you find him the same way you find the rest of your Buyers: in *LMP,* by the titles he's previously packaged and sold, through the trade press, through your professional network of contacts and connections. You approach him the same way, too: with a well-written outline, proposal, and sample, which is similar in as many respects as possible in style, tone, subject, or format to books he's already successfully packaged and sold.

SUMMING UP THE BOOK BUYER'S MARKETPLACE

Finding the right Buyer for your Product is essential to getting it published. The right Buyer may be a large trade publisher, an independent, a packager, or a specialty house (mass market, small press, regional, religious, children's, etc.). The right option for you might be to be your own Buyer and self-publish or to find a subsidy or sponsorship. The right option is almost never a vanity publisher. Once you've indentified the Buyer by general category, you must zero in on the right one for *your* Product, and then actually create that Product.

In my seminars we sometimes do a group exercise in creating a Product, beginning, as in improv theater, with a suggestion from the audience. Here's what the blackboard might look like after we're done:

TOPIC: Jet lag
MEDIUM: Nonfiction book
STYLE: Information—a problem solver
CUSTOMERS: Frequent travelers, especially business
BUYERS: Trade, special-interest (travel), and business publishers

Of course, it's much easier to fill in those blanks with a nonfiction proposal than it is with a novel. Perform this exercise yourself, with your idea, always keeping in mind who your Product's Customer is and through which Buyers in the book trade you will reach him.

SELLING TO HOLLYWOOD, BROADWAY, AND SILICON VALLEY

WRITING FOR HOLLYWOOD

There are three ways to sell your writing to films or television. One is to sell the theatrical rights to your previously published book or article to a producer, studio, or network for adaptation to the screen. Another is to produce a script—your own original story or an adaptation of someone else's, to which you have secured theatrical rights—and sell that to an independent producer or studio. A third is to come up with a marketable idea (in the jargon of the film business, a "high concept") and sell the rights to develop it into a Product (a script) to a producer, network, or studio.

It is much easier to sell your writing to publishers at a distance of thousands of miles from the publishing capital of the country than it is to market your Products to film or television without ever setting foot in tinsel town. You must know even more about how the industry works to gain entrée to the market in film than you must in publishing. Though all the techniques that tune you into the Information Ozone in publishing can and should be employed in your film Buyer research, there is no substitute for firsthand experience of how Hollywood works, or for having information sources in the business. It is sometimes possible to create and cultivate those sources via phone and mail, but because what Buyers in this market want changes so rapidly, inside information is worth its weight in popcorn.

Established film writers insist that an agent is an absolute necessity for a screenwriter. Producers are even warier than publishers about reading unsolicited material because the risk of lawsuits is so great and the financial stakes so high. That doesn't mean your chances of selling an unagented screenplay or even an idea or proposal are impossible—just very, very slim, and slimmer still if you are geographically removed from the hub of the film universe. If you are a celebrity, or even someone with a very unusual personal story—for example, if you've just shot a diet doctor, beaten an addiction to hard drugs, or walked on the moon—you may be able to sell it to films. Then the producers will come to you because they want your story. And if you're still alive and not hopelessly entangled in preparing your book on the subject or getting out of jail, you may be able to make a deal. Or if you are a nonfiction writer with an option on the rights to a topical story that television networks want for a movie of the week, you can sell an idea without ever writing a screenplay.

We'll get to that. But first, let's review the marketing rules learned in the previous chapters of this book. They apply here, even though the jargon is different. The Buyer is the producer, studio, or agent (and in some cases, the Talent); the Customer is the network or distributor; the Product is the filmscript or proposal (the synopsis and treatment). Because movies and television productions cost so much, Products are usually purchased in stages, with money being added to the project as each stage is successfully completed and the Buyer's Buyer, who is also his Customer, underwrites the next stage of the Product development.

Is that clear? Probably not, unless you're already familiar with the process by which films are created as well as how they are sold. And if you're not and are trying to write for the small or large screen, you'd better go out right now and buy yourself a good book that explains the whole process. That's the first step in market research. Once you understand the process, you'll see how the same steps that apply to marketing books and magazine articles apply to marketing for the screen. Identify the Buyer and the Customer. Learn what their needs and problems are. Give them a Product that meets their needs and solves their problems.

Briefly, most Hollywood deals are made using other people's money. Production money usually comes to a producer from either a network or a movie studio, though sometimes outside funds are raised. Because that's the financial chain, most writers who manage to get their books purchased for film don't write the finished product, at least not their first few times out. Producers simply buy the rights to their material and hire a writer with film credentials to write the script—a "bankable" writer, someone whom networks or studios trust and admire. If the Buyer wants your book strongly enough, you may have the leverage required to demand an opportunity to co-write or otherwise help develop the final script. If this happens, you will be paid additional money for your work, at rates set by the Screenwriters Guild.

If, on the other hand, you are trying to market original screenplays, you must understand the requirements of the genre well enough to produce a professional-looking synopsis, treatment, and script, although with every project you may not get to the final stage. Experienced screenwriters have Products in various stages of development with as many potential Buyers as they can find at any one

time. Some don't feel there's much sense in completing a
script before the market has been tested—before a producer has expressed interest in or offered money for the
synopsis and treatment. That certainly is in line with my
thinking. If you've sold to films before or depend on them
for a living, you may have several ideas out in "turn-
around," as the stage of waiting for conditional approval
before proceeding to finished script is called. Even so, I
think it's a good idea to have completed at least one
screenplay before you try to market the synopsis and
treatment, just to know that you can do it and to have
something to show a Buyer who wants evidence of your
ability to complete a script.

There are three different television markets for writers.
One is episodic television (comedy and drama), another is
television movies, and the third is documentary program-
ming. Although much of the latter is generated in-house
through network news departments, some is produced by
television documentary makers and underwritten by networks.

Because of the threat of lawsuits, those producers who
are in the market for work by newcomers will not even
open an unsolicited manuscript or read an outline, treatment, or synopsis without a legal document to protect
them from potential lawsuits, theft, plagiarism, etc.—a
release from liability. On page 89 there is a sample legal
release form, some variation of which is required by almost every producer, network, or studio. Some kind of
release should accompany your synopsis, treatment, or
script if it does not have the imprimatur of an agent.
Without such a release, your Product will be returned,
unopened, by your Buyer. It is a far better idea to write a
careful query letter to your Buyer and include in it the
information that you will sign his particular release or a
standard release form. That query letter should indicate,
if you are writing for an existing series, that you are familiar with the show and its themes and characters, that you
have one or more ideas that seem appropriate for the

show, that you have a synopsis, treatment, or script and want to submit it for consideration on a speculative basis.

Yes, I know I've warned against writing on spec. But in television, unless you're an experienced writer with a good reputation and a lot of screen credits, that's the only way to get an assignment to a particular show or for a particular movie of the week. Still, since Buyers purchase at each stage of development from treatment through finished script, you may not develop every marketable idea to its final stage until there is a Buyer ready to pay for it.

Your query letter will elicit a flat rejection or a request for the treatment and/or script. If you have researched your Product as well as your market, you know how to write the treatment; if not, learn—by any means possible. Most synopses are one page or less; treatments range from five to ten pages. In *The Complete Book of Scriptwriting,* one of the best how-to references in the field, J. Michael Straczynski defines the differences this way: "Whereas the synopsis indicates that a certain group of characters interact, a treatment deals more extensively with how they interact. It gives a more accurate feeling for the way characters move, speak, and act . . . and includes a reasonable amount of dialogue." A script's length depends on the format—the half-hour or one-hour episode, the two-hour movie, or the one-hour or half-hour documentary.

Television Buyers usually option a script or idea only after they have some indication that a network is interested in buying it. They then may make a development deal that in effect underwrites a producer's execution of the script—other peoples' money at work again. Your Buyers are production companies, which are listed by name, address, and other identifying criteria in the directories favored by the industry: the *Pacific Coast Studio Directory* (6331 Hollywood Boulevard, Hollywood CA 90028) and the *Scriptwriter's Marketplace* (6715 Sunset Boulevard, Hollywood CA 90028). These and other sources tell what producers are looking for, which depends, of course, on what the networks want. In "other sources," inside information—the kind made available to producers and agents by the networks themselves—is best. That information sometimes seeps into the trade press, and other times is given only to established writers. It also changes so rapidly (as do the people in charge at the networks) that last month's memo is today's exhausted cliché. Here are typical excerpts from such memos:

> Today, the head of series for the network indicated that they are primarily looking for an 8 o'clock action-adventure. They would also like to develop a western and a period adventure show. They are eager to hear unusual formats in any area except medical, lawyer, cop, private eye, espionage or airline shows. They would also like to develop two half-hour action-adventure dramas with humor.

Here is another:

> This week the network indicated for midseason that it is primarily looking for action-adventure shows and shows with urban youth appeal for possible 9 o'clock Wednesday, Friday and Saturday time slots. It is not interested in medical or western shows. It emphasized strong character shows with wit and humor and indicated an interest in developing shows for female leads.

What these memos make clear is that Customers have very definite ideas, and Buyers must be prepared to offer Products that meet their demands. Sometimes up-to-date market information will tell you what a producer is looking for; sometimes you may spot a trend and bring it to a producer's attention, particularly if it is a theme or idea for a series that is a logical fit for that series. The best way to identify your Buyer for a particular series is to watch the post-show credit roll and see who produces it for which production company. Then contact that company with a query letter indicating that you have a concept, synopsis, treatment, and script appropriate for the series and wish to submit it along with a release form. You must pique the producer's curiosity by telling him that you have an idea but not specifically disclosing it; thus your query letter should sound confident, knowledgeable, and competent as well as intriguing.

A new series is typically created as a spin-off of a pilot or television movie that is usually two hours in length. The pilot is a way for a Buyer to test-market a series, so producers are looking for movie ideas with series potential. Thus, in trying to sell a new series idea, you must have a treatment or script for a pilot as well as for a series episode in order to interest a producer.

Some magazines and periodicals are routinely scanned by film producers in the hope of finding material that can be adapted for the screen. If you are the writer of such an article, a filmmaker may approach you or contact the publication (or your agent) for rights to the material. Previous publication enhances your credibility. In most cases your talents as a scriptwriter will not be solicited—only your ownership or your option on the material that was the basis of your article. Some magazines have arrangements or channels through which articles of potential interest to filmmakers are negotiated for screen adaptation through the magazine's own agents. If you have sold only one-time or first serial rights and retained an interest in or total ownership of theatrical rights, they will have to come to you to bargain. If you wrote your article for hire—say, as a newspaper reporter or on-staff magazine writer—the publication generally owns film rights, though the writer is usually compensated for a film sale.

As a freelance writer who produces a feature story on a person for a magazine or for film, you must own or otherwise control rights to the principal's story before you can negotiate a film sale. Often you can option such rights for a small fee. Such an agreement will invariably provide the principal with compensation if the script or treatment is ever sold. Options of this sort are frequently negotiated on what is called, in the business, an "if come" basis—if it gets purchased, the money comes to you, and you pay the principal. If it doesn't, you are out only the cost of the option.

Owning the rights to a topical or newsworthy story helps you negotiate with your Buyer. Even if you didn't write the original story of, say, a housewife held prisoner by alien invaders or a hermit who survived the eruption of a volcano, you may still be able to option the rights by contacting the principal. The writer of that story has no ownership of such rights unless he has previously negotiated for them. This is where a writer most often collaborates, financially, on a fifty-fifty basis. If you have based your concept or script on a published article, your own or someone else's, include printed clips with your treatment and synopsis or with your query letter. But remember, these are extras—you still need a synopsis and a treatment showing how you propose to develop a story or script from this brief material. You must still turn the idea into a Product, or at least go through the initial stages, which indicate its worthiness for film adaptation.

Writing a query letter that intrigues a Buyer without giving your idea away is tricky. But sending a synopsis, treatment, or script without some indication that a Buyer is interested is often futile. Still, if you feel that only a synopsis or treatment can do your idea justice, include your signed release with it, or don't bother. And register your Product with the Writers Guild of America, West, for your own protection from plagiarism, just as you include a release for the protection of the Buyer. You do this by sending a copy of the script and a fee (ten dollars as of this writing) to the Guild at 8955 Beverly Boulevard, Los Angeles, CA 90048. Write "Registered, WGAw" on your material. This backup is absolutely essential in case there is a question of ownership. The serial number the WGAw assigns your material is proof that it is, indeed, your own work.

In a different category of possible Buyers is a star for whom you may have created a television or film script. You can and may approach that star personally (well, somewhat) by writing to him or her in care of the Screen Actors Guild at 7750 Sunset Boulevard, Los Angeles, CA 90046, which forwards such mail directly to the performer. If that person is interested, he can either option your Product or purchase it outright; he can raise the money to produce it through his own sources (very big stars sometimes do this); or he can make his deals with the networks or studios. This is a chancy way to sell a script, but some writers have been successful.

Just as there are book packagers, there are film packagers. The large agencies that handle literary, theatrical, and entertainment talent are the best-known packagers. They attempt to sell a film package to a studio or network by using as many of their star-quality writers, directors, and actors as possible. If you are represented by one of these agencies or can gain access to someone at International Creative Management or William Morris Agency, to name the largest, a packager might also be a potential Buyer for your film, television or stage play.

THE MOVIE MARKET

Selling original movie scripts is even harder than selling teleplays—the risks are greater, the figures are breathtaking, and the deals exceedingly complex. Once again, the role of the agent cannot be understated. Most film scripts don't get beyond a junior story editor if they come in without agency representation. But if you do decide to approach a Buyer on your own, make sure you have researched him thoroughly, know the kind of material he usually produces, and are certain that your work is similar in type, style, and, especially, budget to what is currently in the Buyer's inventory. While the major studios have been the only Buyers for very expensive films, they too are now beginning to look for profitable opportunities in low-budget films.

One additional channel for reaching a film Buyer is through an entertainment lawyer. Many of these professionals put film packages together much as the large entertainment agencies do, with initial financing and sometimes public offerings to finance independent productions, or make development deals with networks, studios, or distributors. These attorneys deal mostly with established film writers, although occasionally they will option a script by a novice on an "if come" basis.

Finding that all-important Hollywood (and, sometimes, New York) agent is not easy. To interest one in handling you, you must have a completed script or own rights to an adaptable book or magazine article. It's hard to interest an agent in a treatment unless you have a finished script. In the appropriate directories, from *LMP* to *Screenwriters Marketplace,* you'll find lists of film agents and information as to what kind of material they want and at what stage of completion they will look at it. Use the same techniques to find a film agent as you would to find a literary agent. And if you already have a literary agent, investigate his relationships with sources in Hollywood.

Because the film world is so small, I don't recommend multiple submissions of film synopses, treatments, or completed scripts. Something that has been shopped indiscriminately to an untargeted group of potential Buyers becomes familiar to many of them before they've even seen it, simply because an agent or another Buyer has mentioned seeing and rejecting it. Usually your query letter will elicit a response of some kind within weeks. Response to a treatment takes longer, as it must go through several echelons at the Buyer's establishment, from story editor to division chief (i.e., the head of a series or the chief of cable movies, etc.). And it must also go to the Buyer's Customer—the producer's network or studio—before the writer is even encouraged to proceed. Payment for treatment, outline, first drafts, and completed scripts is determined by union scale; the Writers Guild, West, can tell you what those scale rates are. And yes, they are ridiculously high, particularly when compared to, say, an advance for a first novel. Also, because the figures are so astronomical, the old truism holds, even truer in films than in books: many are seen, but few are chosen.

If film is your chosen medium, what I've told you here is only a fraction of what you need to know about the industry, how it works, and what's required of you. Now go to your specific industry sources, to that Information Ozone, for details.

While you're courting producers, studios, and agents, don't neglect other potential Buyers. These include contests, scholarships, special programs, and internships designed by the industry to encourage new talent. They exist not only in movies and television, but also in a broadcast medium often neglected by writers—radio drama. The resurgence of talk radio in the recent past has spawned a need for talented writers in this medium. Approach your Buyers here the same way you approach film producers: through the appropriate professional outlets, including existing radio series and other producers who program for this market.

If you are interested in writing for radio, you should know that there are two kinds of outlets—public radio and noncommercial radio. Many producers can be identified by the simple process of calling your local station or network affiliate and asking the program manager for the name and address of the producer. *Writer's Digest* magazine also carries occasional reports of radio drama producers looking for new material. Once you've identified your Buyer, prepare your query letter, synopsis, treatment, and script, using all the market data you've been able to gather on what Buyers need and all the professionalism you've acquired by learning the form and medium from available samples and teaching materials, and do your best.

WRITING FOR THE STAGE

There are two ways to sell stage plays. One is through a playbook publisher, who may specialize in children's plays suitable for school productions, religious plays, or ethnic plays. Publishers of contemporary plays also purchase scripts for their market, but to get these plays published, it is necessary to get them produced. And that is the second way to sell a stage play—to sell the performance rights to a theatrical producer.

Community and local theaters of varying quailty and levels of professionalism pay minimal fees for performance rights; the only playwrights who earn more than a token amount are those whose works are produced on the legitimate stage or are adapted for film or television production. But many small theaters have programs designed to encourage new playwright talent and have some small budgets set aside for this. If your play is produced by a local or regional theater with a good reputation, it may have a chance of making it to Broadway or, more often, to Off or Off-Off Broadway. Even at that professional level, the financial rewards for most playwrights are not great; compared to film or television, the stage is a poor relation, even if the Product is of much greater quality. Again, connections in your industry will be the most useful to you as a playwright: the artistic director of your local community theater, the drama department of your university, the open competitions sponsored by theaters, such as the O'Neill summer program or the Humana Festival at the Actors Theatre of Louisville.

So much of the writing in plays depends on the actual

staging of them that this is simply the only way to perfect a script. But the initial stages of marketing a play script to a Buyer—producer or artistic director or competition manager—are similar to the approaches you would make to a book, magazine, or film Buyer. Once again, know your Buyer and your Customer, know their needs and problems, and give them a Product that meets their needs and solves their problems. Find the best sources of information and make the connections you must have. Provide professionally written material in the appropriate style or format, supply supporting market data where available and logical, and state a reason to buy—for instance, that the particular regional theater you've approached has an established process for showcasing the work of local playwrights or that the subject of your play matches the kind of audience the theater usually attracts.

SELLING TO STAGE, SCREEN, AND IN BETWEEN: A SUMMARY

In writing for films, television, radio, or the theater, professionalism is even more important than it is in the periodical or book trade. The financial commitment is so great that producers are simply unwilling to waste time and money dealing with someone who doesn't know the parameters, the market requirements, and the form, from the query letter to the completed script, as well as the players—the artistic director, the story editor, the dramaturge or literary manager who gives first reading to the unsolicited play script. In this chapter I've outlined some of these things and ignored others; specifically, I have not included samples of synopses, scripts, outlines, etc. For these, you should read original sources—every film script, teleplay, or play script you can get your hands on. You should study the how-to materials available for each medium. And if a Buyer bites, you should negotiate only with the assistance of a real pro—an agent if you have one, a lawyer even if you also have an agent. The stakes are high, especially in Hollywood, and the loopholes are many and indecipherable to anyone but a real expert.

Once again, don't send *anything* to a stage or screen Buyer without a release unless you want to be tagged as an amateur. Here is a sample release form:

Gentlemen:

1. I am submitting to your herewith the following material (hereinafter referred to as "said material"):

   TITLE:_____

   FORM OF MATERIAL (e.g., screenplay, treatment, novel, play):_____

   _____

   PRINCIPAL CHARACTERS:_____

   _____

   BRIEF SUMMARY OF THEME OR PLOT:_____

   _____

   _____

   _____

   _____

   WGA REGISTRATION NO.:_____

   NUMBER OF PAGES:_____

2. I request that you read and evaluate said material, and you hereby agree to do so, and if I subsequently make a written request, you agree to advise me of your decision with respect to the material.

3. I warrant that I am the sole owner and author of said material, that I have the exclusive right and authority to submit

the same to you upon the terms and conditions stated herein, and that all of the important features of said material are summarized herein. I will indemnify you of and from any and all claims, loss or liability (including reasonable attorneys' fees) that may be asserted against you, or incurred by you, at any time in connection with said material, or any use thereof.

4. I agree that any part of said material which does not in itself constitute protectible literary property may be used by you without any liability to me, and that nothing in this agreement nor the fact of my submission of said material to you shall be deemed to place you in any different position than anyone else to whom I have not submitted said material with respect to any portion of said material which does not constitute protectible literary property.

5. I understand that you do not purchase literary properties as a general rule, and that if you were to do so, you would purchase said material through the established channels in the industry and not through a submission such as this. I recognize that you have access to and/or may create or have created literary materials and ideas which may be similar or identical to said material in theme, idea, plot, format, or other respects. I agree that I will not be entitled to any compensation because of the use by you of any such similar or identical material which may have been independently created by you or may have come to you from any other independent source. I understand that no confidential relationship is established by my submitting the material to you hereunder.

6. I understand that you have adopted the policy, with respect to the unsolicited submission of material, of refusing to accept, consider, or evaluate unsolicited material unless the person submitting such material has signed an agreement in a form substantially the same as this agreement. I specifically acknowledge that you would refuse to accept, consider, or otherwise evaluate my material in the absence of my acceptance of each and all of the provisions hereof. I shall retain all right to submit this or similar material to persons other than you.

7. You agree that if you use any legally protectible portion of said material, provided it has not been obtained by you from, or independently created by, another source, you will pay me an amount which is comparable to the compensation normally paid by you for similar material or an amount equal to the fair market value thereof as of the date of this agreement, whichever is greater. If we are unable to agree as to said amount, or in the event of any dispute concerning any alleged use of said material (e.g., whether you have used legally protectible portions thereof), or any other dispute arising out of or in connection with said material or with reference to this agreement, its validity, construction, performance, nonperformance, operation, breach, continuance or termination, such dispute shall be submitted to arbitration. Each party hereby waives any and all rights and benefits which he or it might otherwise have or be entitled to under the laws of _____ to litigate any such dispute in court, it being the intention of the parties to arbitrate, according to the provisions hereof, all such disputes. Either party (either you or I) may commence arbitration proceedings by giving the other party written notice thereof and in such notices designating one arbitrator. Within twenty (20) days after receipt of such notice, the other party shall designate in writing another arbitrator. If the other party shall fail or refuse, for whatever reason, to select a second arbitrator, within twenty (20) days, as aforesaid, then the first arbitrator appointed shall serve as the sole arbitrator and shall promptly determine the controversy. The two arbitrators shall promptly select a third arbitrator, and if they cannot agree on a third arbitrator within ten (10) days after the appointment of the second arbitrator, either party may secure appointment of the third arbitrator, by application to the American Arbitration Association. Each of the arbitrators shall be a person experienced and knowledgeable in the entertainment industry. The arbitrators, when appointed, shall promptly determine the controversy by majority vote and such determination shall be final and each of the parties shall be bound thereby. The arbitration shall be conducted in the County of _____, State of _____, and, except as herein expressly provided otherwise, the arbitration shall be governed by and subject to the laws of the State of _____

and the then prevailing rules of the American Arbitration Association. The arbitrators' decision shall be controlled by the terms of this agreement, and I agree that the amount of any award shall be an amount which is comparable to the compensation normally paid by you for similar material or an amount equal to the fair market value thereof as of the date of this agreement, whichever is greater. If either party shall fail to appear at the hearing on the date designated in accordance with the rules of the American Arbitration Association, or shall otherwise fail to participate in the arbitration proceedings, then the arbitrators or arbitrator, as the case may be, are empowered to proceed ex parte.

8. Either party to this agreement may assign or license its or his rights hereunder, but such assignment or license shall not relieve such party of his or its obligations hereunder. It is agreed that this agreement shall inure to the benefit of the parties hereto and their heirs, successors, representatives, assigns and licensees, and that any such heir, successor, representative, assign or licensee shall be deemed a third party beneficiary under this agreement.

9. I have retained at least one copy of said material, and I hereby release you of any and all liability for loss of, or damage to, the copies of said material submitted to you hereunder.

10. I enter into this agreement with the express understanding that you agree to read and evaluate said material in express reliance upon this agreement and my convenants, representations and warranties contained herein, and that in the absence of such an agreement, you would not read or evaluate said material.

11. I hereby state that I have read and understand this agreement and that no oral representations of any kind have been made to me, and that this agreement states our entire understanding with reference to the subject matter hereof. Any modification or waiver of any of the provisions of this agreement must be in writing and signed by both of us.

12. If more than one party signs this agreement as submittor, then references to "I" or "me" throughout this agreement shall apply to each such party, jointly or severally.

13. Should any provision or part of any provision be void or unenforceable, such provision or part thereof shall be deemed omitted and this agreement with such provision or part thereof omitted shall remain in full force and effect. This agreement shall at all times be construed so as to carry out the purposes hereof.

DATED:_____   Very truly yours,

_____
Signature

_____
Print Name

_____
Address

_____
City and State

_____
Telephone Number

THE SOFTWARE MARKET

As personal computers have come within the financial range of a larger number of consumers, the software marketplace has opened up a whole new Buyer's market for those innovative publishers seeking to combine new technology and books. As the personal computer market goes through its own upheavals, standardization is the rule; the software that runs on the most popular machines will capture the major share of the market.

Software writers are the programmers, authors, and inventors of computer programs that help computer owners play games, solve problems, or perform business-related functions efficiently. Although most software companies—Buyers—originate many programs in-house, there is a growing market for freelancers who have the particular skills needed to create software that serves their market.

This is not a market that should be approached by anyone who lacks technological skill or fluency in turning an idea suitable for a computer into a Product. The specifications for submitting your work to a software publisher vary; some want an outline and complete documentation with a submission, others will only respond to a query letter, while some require a demo disk. Some publish programmer guidelines, others disseminate information on what is desired through magazines, computer networks, industry newsletters, and reference guides.

The best way to identify your Buyer is to be familiar with the programs and the type of equipment typical of his Product, because your Product must fit an existing line. While the *1984 Programmer's Market* is your best guide to potential markets, *Writer's Market* also carries a good listing of Buyers. Like scriptwriting, this is a writer's market that demands total proficiency in form and creativity in content. Most software is purchased on a royalty basis, and it is important to know exactly what rights—nonexclusive, machine specific, or irrevocable—you are selling with your software.

Some major software producers are moving into trade book publishing. Microsoft, whose MS-DOS operating system runs IBM's personal computer as well as those of about fifty other hardware manufacturers, was the first to spin off a trade book publishing division specializing in computer books, with an established channel for distribution to the book trade through the electronic publishing division of Simon & Schuster. Thus the company can support its newest technology, its software, with manuals and other books—with the printed word. Prognosticators expect this to start a new trend in which the marriage of technology and publishing spawns a specialty publisher with two ways to market products: through machines and their owners, and through books and other communications media targeted to those owners.

So if you can create software and also explain, describe, teach, or amplify it with the written word, you may be able to publish it for both appropriate technologies, books and machines. Use the same basic marketing techniques that have been described elsewhere in this book: plenty of research, good lines into the industry's Information Ozone, and a marketer's highly developed feel for this growing market. Understand the requirements of the medium, follow them, and don't forget the Theory of Looking Backward—it probably applies here more than to any other area of writing, creating, and selling. For more information on creating and marketing software, including how to negotiate contracts with purchasing companies, see *The Complete Software Marketplace* by Roger Hoffman (Warner Software/Warner Books).

WRITING THE SELLING PROPOSAL

A book or magazine proposal must stimulate, move, excite, or awe a Buyer. It does any or all of these things because of the personal connection it makes with him, on the basis of subject matter and, occasionally, the quality of the writing.

The first thing your proposal must do is make a Buyer jump out of his seat with excitement. Touch a nerve somewhere in him. Make him want to publish your Product. Give him the right instincts.

But your proposal must also convince your Buyer to act on his instincts by providing what he needs to convince others above him in the publishing hierarchy. You convince a Buyer by showing him that your Product will service his market, balance his issue or book list, return his investment with money and recognition.

THE BOOK PROPOSAL

A book proposal does not get a Buyer on his feet by being cutesy or by arriving in his office with some gimmick, like a jack-in-the-box, an exploding cigar, or a stripper (real examples for books on junk food, how to stop smoking, and old-time vaudeville stars)—every editor in the business has his own illustrations of this surprisingly prevalent form of oversell. A gimmick is a diversion, and is almost never useful or appropriate when trying to sell your Buyer. Some time ago a story appeared on the wire services about a writer who threatened to cut off his right arm if a publisher did not agree to at least look at his book proposal. Enough publishers felt enough remorse to look, but, as far as I know, not one bought. What is memorable about that incident is the right arm, not the book, just as some ads are memorable because they're cute or funny or striking, but at the expense of the product. So don't let delivery of your sales message get in the way of your Product.

Your proposal must first of all indicate that you are aware of your Buyer's needs. It must contain the evidence he needs to make him act on his instinct to purchase. That is, you must show him that your Product is useful or interesting to his Customers, will earn him money (or at least not lose him his investment), and gain him recognition in his market and in his organization. You do this by creating a proposal that:

1. Explains the Product.
2. Identifies the market.
3. Establishes your credentials or level of expertise.

Your proposal should answer these questions for your Buyer: What is this all about? Who cares? Why is this writer qualified to produce it? That, in essence, is the organization of a good proposal. Each year a busy editor at a trade publishing house sees close to 5000 proposals of varying lengths and in various forms—conversation, outline, sample. Some go immediately into the circular file (the wastebasket) because it's clear that the subject is of no interest to the Buyer or has little commercial or aesthetic appeal, or because the proposal indicates that the writer cannot do justice to the material—can't even, in some sorry cases, write a simple declarative sentence.

Let's consider the first topic, explaining the Product. In most cases you do this in a sentence or two in the letter that accompanies your proposal or in the query that precedes it. All this short paragraph does is tell what kind of Product you have, fiction or nonfiction, essay or article, and what it's about, as in *"War and Peace* is a prose epic about the Napoleonic Wars," or *"In Search of Excellence* is a nonfiction book about the best-run corporations in America." In the initial paragraph of the longer proposal this explanation will be expanded to convey more information about how you propose to treat this topic ("While on one level *Moby Dick* is a thrilling adventure story about the attempt to capture a great white whale, it is also an allegory about man's relation to the universe") and what you have to say about it *("In Search of Excellence* defines those eight basic practices characteristic of successfully managed companies"). This part of your proposal may also sketch your methodology or approach to your subject in a nonfiction proposal, or, in fiction, may include relevant information about setting, plot, and character.

The second step is to address the question of who cares. This is where your market information goes, as does pertinent material about books similar to yours that have been successful and ways in which your book is different (more complete, more specialized, more general, a humorous rather than a serious approach, etc.). This is not the place to give a complete critique of other books; it is simply a guide to positioning or an image, for the Buyer, of his potential Customers ("Everyone who bought *Thin Thighs in Thirty Days* will want *Five Days to Firmer Jowls"*).

If statistics help buttress your proposal ("Twenty thousand card-carrying members of the Edsel Owners Association, all of whom can be reached via association publications, make up the potential audience for *A Mis-*

take to Remember"), use them. Even in a fiction proposal you can position your material according to genre (*"Pitcher in the Pumpernickle,* the story of the coming of age of Herschel Levine, a sensitive, perpetually horny adolescent from Passaic, is in the tradition of classic American fiction"), style, subject matter, or potential Customer ("I think the increasing number of romance readers will be interested in *Lust's Labors Lost,* whose heroine embodies the passionate, headstrong, independent woman who appeals to so many readers who made your last twelve dozen Foxy Publishers titles best-sellers"). This is the trickiest part of your proposal to frame because it is the one that must convey your enthusiasm for and intelligence about your work. Thus it is easy to oversell by making extravagant claims or to undersell by making defensive comments like "Of course, this is just a rough idea," which indicate that you are not confident that your work can stand up to the promises you make for it.

If you have pertinent market data, use it in this section. If you don't but can position the idea in some way that helps the Buyer imagine a Customer for it, or tells him how it would fit on his list or why he is exactly the right Buyer for it ("I know that you have a particular interest in craft books and have developed an audience for them"), do that. The phrase to be careful of is "No one has ever written a book like this before. You could be the first publisher to recognize the real need that exists for *How to Live with a Man-eating Plant,*" and other variations on that theme. If no one ever did it before, few Buyers are going to risk much, if any, money on it now.

The third step in your proposal is simple; if you have credits, credentials, or clips, use them. If you have experience relevant to the topic of your book ("I lived for five years on the deserted Pacific island which is the setting for *Over the Horizon"*) or titles or background in the subject, use them. If you have nothing to say except "I am a writer from Ulan Bator who has never been published; this is my first novel," say that. Ultimately, the work speaks for itself. But only after the important question—what's in it for your Buyer?—has been answered.

This is how a proposal might look at this stage—in fact, this was the first draft proposal for the book you are reading right now.

How to Sell What You Write is a guide to marketing the written word. Although it is aimed at the professional writer, its practical advice, offered in a direct, readable style, will be of even greater value to beginning and amateur writers who are trying to get published for the first time, move from specialized to general markets, expand from local or regional to national audiences, or simply earn more money with their writing skills. How to Sell What You Write will help them accomplish these goals through effective, proven marketing techniques.

While this subject has been partially or sporadically covered in the trade and specialty publishing market as well as in many periodicals, no other treatment of it approaches the task primarily from a marketing perspective. How to Sell What You Write is based on this principle: selling the written word is, in several important respects, analogous to selling any other product—bread, soap, or life insurance. It guides the writer through the process of generating ideas, creating marketable products, identifying appropriate buyers, and making sales of magazine articles, nonfiction books, novels, films, radio and play scripts, and even software manuals. It describes the process of combining writing skills with marketing expertise for maximum effectiveness and profitability.

How to Sell What You Write is the distillation of a bestselling author and journalist's successful seminars of the same name, in which she has taught her proven techniques to hundreds of writers. Jane

Adams brings impressive professional credentials and an established reputation as a selling writer to this important, useful book; unlike any other writer in this field, she has a national reputation based on four published books, both fiction and nonfiction, and over a hundred published articles in national magazines and newspapers.

This brief proposal was accompanied by a writing sample—the first chapter of this book—and an annotated outline of succeeding chapters. And forty-eight hours after it was seen by the publisher for whom it was specifically designed, a sale was made.

While the foregoing may be useful to you as a guide, it should not be taken as a step-by-step blueprint for your own proposal, which may be longer or shorter or contain more or less market data and more or less author identification. And I'm not going to tell you whether your proposal should be single- or double-spaced, fit on one page, or be bound in precious gems. Those things don't matter. What *does* matter is that you write as concisely as possible with as much or as little information needed to get the primary message across: what your book, article, or script is about, who wants to know, how it is like or different from what currently exists in the market, and why you're the best person to write it. Then you clean and polish and clarify and edit your proposal, making sure that every word counts and that there aren't so many of them that your Buyer is overwhelmed and must take six aspirin before he even starts reading it. Remember, the Buyer who's reading your proposal is overworked, underpaid, and not really expecting to find something to make him leap out of his chair and count his Christmas bonus in his slush pile, in proposals addressed specifically to him, or even in submissions coming under the imprimatur of an agent. Your proposal must overcome his dismal expectations and move him to do something—even if it's only to turn the page and read your sample chapters.

In my conferences with clients, I read only the proposal, and never more than two pages of that, plus the first page of a manuscript or writing sample. I limit my reading to this not only because I am basically lazy, but also because that's the same amount of attention most writers get from Buyers, unless the Buyer has solicited the proposal, of course, in which case most will read it through to the final word.

If you can't sell it in one page, you can't sell it. And if in that one page you don't address your Buyer's immediate question—what's in this for me?—he'll read no further. You have only one chance to capture his attention, and the best way to do that is to put your primary selling message right up front.

If you're one of those writers who takes twenty pages to get to the point, fine; take the first nineteen pages, condense them to a paragraph, and throw them away. If your excuse for not doing this is that you can write the book, article, or script but you can't write *about* it, you'd better learn how. Because if you don't, no one will ever read the book you've written or are planning to write.

While brevity is important, many books call for more of an explanation or description that can be squeezed onto one page. If this is true of yours, make sure that the first page contains the most important and relevant information, and indicate that additional pages include other pertinent material: a more complete professional *vita*, for example ("Attached is a list of my publishing credits") or a complete market breakdown ("Included is an excerpt from the *Annual Report of The Pulse of the Nation*, which indicates where and in what substantial numbers potential readers of this book exist").

Sometimes your proposal will generate a request for more information, material, or an additional writing sample. When it does, you know you've interested your Buyer. But don't expect at the outset that this will happen: make sure you've anticipated and answered every essential question your Buyer must and will raise: what's this about? who cares? why should this person write this manuscript? and what's in it for me?

There is no foolproof formula for a successful proposal. I could offer samples of dozens of different ones; some would be acceptable to some Buyers and not to others. If you've targeted your proposal so closely to one Buyer that if it doesn't work for him, it won't work for another, you may have to revise it extensively before submitting it elsewhere. If you've made it so vague that a Buyer can't position it clearly enough to distinguish it from dozens of other books on his list, you may have to rewrite it to demonstrate how well it does, in fact, meet the needs you've identified him as having. That's what a good proposal does: It gives a Buyer all the information he needs to evaluate a Product in terms of what needs it meets and what problems it solves for him.

If you follow the steps I've outlined here in creating your proposal, you'll notice that the Product itself is taking clearer shape in your own mind. For me, writing a proposal is the first step in preparing to write. It establishes my direction, market, style, tone, and format. It tells me whether my material is really suited to my medium, too. Sometimes what I thought was a book idea was really only sufficient for a magazine article, or what I first conceived as an article turned out to be worth the effort and research required for a book. As the requirements of the proposal form force me to define its most salient and marketable points, I begin to shape the actual Product and prepare my writing sample.

A word here about samples. Many professional writers resist Buyers' demands for writing samples. They think writing on speculation is beneath them, that unpaid work is wasted, particularly since publishers all think they publish too many books already and often seem to be looking for reasons to cut back on the number they produce. These writers feel that a proposal should contain a description, an outline, some marketing information, and a list of their publishing credits.

Good for them, and may they learn the error of their ways quickly. My feeling is that there are thousands of terrific writers—you, the reader, for one—who would be delighted, not insulted, to write a sample chapter or two if that's what it takes to sell their Product. They're willing to count those hours as overhead, the cost of doing business as a writer, and understand that they can and will get paid, eventually, for what they've done. By providing the Buyer with a strong sample, you indicate your enthusiasm for and dedication to your Product. I have written at least a brief sample for every book I've sold and never felt it was beneath me, even though I have an extensive list of publishing credits. I believe a Buyer has a right to see what he's going to get, to have solid evidence that a writer can do a credible job with his material. And if you can't, the sample you create will tell you, before you have to hear those words from a Buyer and destroy the credibility you've gained by a good idea and a well-written proposal. As Nan Talese, editor in chief of a major trade publisher, said in the *Authors Guild Bulletin,* "It's not that we can't imagine a book on the basis of just a proposal—it's all too easy to imagine the book. Unfortunately, it may not be the book the author is going to write."

THE MAGAZINE PROPOSAL

Most magazines do not require a writing sample, though they will welcome a list of published credits and an offer to send samples on request. A letter usually serves as the proposal itself, and the letter, no more than two pages in total, follows the same basic format as a book proposal: It identifies the subject, describes the market, and establishes the writer. It also includes the approximate length of the article, when it can be delivered, and if it is time dated, as in "'Leftover Handicrafts: Turning Mashed Potatoes into Doorstops' would be appropriate for post-holiday reading."

Magazine writers in my seminars often ask how they can protect their ideas from being stolen by unprincipled editors. Book writers ask me that, too, and my answer is that this is something that seems to happen more than it actually does. Most editors are principled, and if someone you've dealt with turned down the very book or article idea you proposed to him a few months ago and then published a similar version of it recently, that doesn't necessarily mean he stole your idea. Copyrighting your material is always a good idea, and we'll go into that in detail in Chapter 11, but there is not much you can do if it happens to you. Understand that the Information Ozone is open to all, an idea isn't yours until you turn it into a specific Product, very few ideas are totally original, and it's hard to recover actual damages. The best response is to come up with another great idea.

Once you've drafted your proposal, look at the preliminary breakdown of potential magazine Buyers. Study any available guidelines and be sure your proposal matches them in every respect. Some magazines publish their own guidelines; for instance, "We want 500 words for a reader's first person story," from a women's magazine. Ignore written guidelines only at your peril: If an editor has taken pains to describe exactly what he wants and your material is not a very close fit, it will go right into the "reject" file. Which is probably as it should be, no matter how good your Product is—if you can't deal with the limitations imposed by the form, you shouldn't be writing in it. What you should be doing is finding a more appropriate Buyer.

Unless your Product is specifically written to order, choose the best fit between your material and three different Buyers in each of your primary markets—consumer, general, and industry press. Then write an appropriate cover letter or query for each one, modifying the body of the letter—the proposal itself—to fit any expressed requirements or to present any additional information you have that is specific to that Buyer. Remember, the point of this exercise is to match your proposal most clearly to the right Buyer. Out of the nine possible Buyers you've identified, one should be exactly right.

What works for me in selling magazine articles is a telephoned query if I know the editor—"Are you interested in a piece on new sexual options for the Eighties?" If the answer is yes, or even maybe, I follow it with a one- or two-page outline, which serves as the proposal. If I don't know the editor, I combine my query and proposal in one letter. I've sold my books with a marketing package consisting of a cover letter, a two-page (maximum) proposal that answers the Buyer's questions about what's in this for him, an annotated chapter outline, and a sample of one or more book chapters.

What has never worked, for me or any other selling writer, is any proposal that does not consider, word for word, the Buyer's needs and problems; that is clever enough to attract a second look but not strong enough to sustain that initial interest; that is gimmicky but without real substance; and that is anything less than my best writing, informed by my total commitment to, interest in, and enthusiasm for my Product.

THE COVER LETTER AND THE QUERY

The cover letter is sometimes a query, although with magazines it will probably be the proposal as well. Every manuscript needs a cover letter, even a short story. In that cover letter you should identify yourself, introduce your Product clearly and concisely, and do so in a way that tells your Buyer you're capable of turning in a finished, professional Product.

A cover letter should never apologize for a Product, as in "This is just a rough idea of what I have in mind." Wherever possible it should explain why you have chosen this Buyer: "I noted in *Literary Market Place* that you are looking for manuscripts dealing with this subject," for example, or "We met at the writer's conference in Ultima Thule ten years ago and you suggested that I send you my book proposal for *The Sex Life of Killer Bees*," or "I read in *Publishers Weekly* that you are creating a new line of young adult books, and think that *Behind Boarding School Doors*, my novel, will be of great interest to your market."

A query letter is different from a cover letter; it does not "cover" a proposal. Rather, it inquires of a Buyer whether he would be receptive to your subsequent submission of a proposal, outline, or Product. You send a query letter to a Buyer who has stated in *LMP, Writer's Market*, or some other place (a writer's conference, for instance) that he will look at "queries only." When a query is required, it must do the same things your proposal must and will: indicate the topic and form of your work and its potential market, and identify you as a likely candidate for the assignment or contract. It must do this in a letter so brief as to give no appearance of being an actual proposal, when, in fact, that's what it is. It must demonstrate to the Buyer that you are a writer worth considering with a Product worth his time to evaluate.

If you can manage to be graceful, charming, or even witty in your query or cover letter, it will get more than a cursory glance. Many Buyers do not meet writers until after they've purchased their Products, and, in some cases, never meet them at all. Often the only sense they have of what kind of person a writer is is through his work. Still, publishers, like other Buyers, prefer to do business with people they like. So think of your cover letter or, when appropriate, your query, as the beginning of a love affair (in publishing, always the best part!) and be as seductive as you can. The object is to get the Buyer to ask you for a date. And, to carry that analogy further, promising what you can't deliver is as deadly in one milieu as the other, and so is masquerading as someone you're not.

A word about that last. These days, when by one recent estimate as many as one out of three job résumés is specious in some respect, publishers are in a stronger position to investigate than most other Buyers; if a writer says he's done something, they can check just by looking up his publishing credits. And if they pay an advance for something that is not in their estimation worthy of publication when completed, they can not only demand their advance back, they can get it. Although I've said elsewhere in this book that it is often possible to sell a Product before you've created it (particularly in nonfiction), if you have any compelling doubts about your ability to complete a Product, write it before you try to sell it. What you write may not be a finished version, but in a first draft—an absolute necessity in fiction—the strengths and weaknesses of the work are there to be evaluated by you *and* your Buyer. At the very least, have other samples of finished Products, sold or not, to prove to a Buyer that you can sustain the effort and produce what you're promising.

QUERIES, COVERS, AND PROPOSALS: SUMMING UP

Here's a brief description of the difference between queries, covers, and proposals. The query is the first contact, the purpose of which is to introduce yourself and introduce your idea. It asks, simply, are you interested in this story, script, book, or article? A query may be the only opportunity you ever get to interface with a particular Buyer, so it's important to make that contact stimulate him to want more.

In magazine submissions you can usually bypass the query stage and combine the query and proposal in one letter. Often the result is that an editor will contact you, if he is interested, and tell you what else should be included or excluded from the proposed article. Sometimes he will ask you to rewrite a proposal with a restatement of the article as he sees it. The proposal you send him by return mail includes a detailed outline of your article, the terms of payment, the deadline, length, rights offered, and kill fee (compensation paid a writer for a work that was commissioned but not accepted—usually fifteen to twenty-five percent of purchase price), all of which will have been discussed between you prior to this rewrite. His agreement to that letter then serves as a contract for the work.

When the work is completed, send it to the editor with a cover letter that explains what you have enclosed; editors work with many writers at once, and you can't expect them to always remember whom they assigned to what. Include in that letter the names and addresses of your sources, if any, to make life easier for your editor and fact checker. Also include an explanation, if necessary, of how the finished article differs from what was expected. If that is the case—if, for example, your research led you to conclude that your original theory was full of holes, or if you've found an unexpected angle to the piece—you will have phoned your editor during the writing process to discuss those changes. And if you agreed on them, restate the points in your cover letter just to remind him of your conversation.

Book queries are not proposals, although they should still address a Buyer's primary questions: What's this about, who cares, what's it like that is already on the market, why are you the best person to write it, and what's in it for him. A simple query at the beginning of the process of turning an idea into a Product can save a great deal of wasted effort, not to mention expenses for photocopying and postage.

Query letters are appropriate when you have no other access or introduction to a potential Buyer and/or when a Buyer has stated that he welcomes queries only. Remember again that this may be your only contact with that particular Buyer, so make your letter direct and complete. The most important point a query letter can make is that you are a pro, even if you've never published a line. That professionalism is implicit when you've targeted the right idea to the appropriate Buyer, explained your subject, theme, and point of view in one or two succinct sentences, and have not either oversold or undersold your Product and your credentials.

If your Buyer says "Queries only," never send a complete manuscript. If he says "proposal and sample," follow those directions precisely. If he says "outline and three chapters," ditto.

I never send complete manuscripts to magazine editors until I've received a letter of agreement or contract, even if, as occasionally happens, the piece is fully written before I attempt to sell it. My experience with these editors is that many of them are secret writers; they want to be involved in the creative process, to have plenty of input and an opportunity to shape the piece as they see fit. So even if the piece is done I break it down into a proposal and outline. Some editors immediately suspect when they see a piece in finished form before agreeing to purchase it that it has been around before it came to them. It may have been, but that is no reason to broadcast that information, as I once did inadvertently by sending *Playgirl* a manuscript that had been assigned and then killed by another magazine. Without even retyping "New Lifestyles, a Cosmo Special Report," I recirculated the rejected manuscript, and even though it was well written and targeted to *Playgirl*'s readers, it bounced back to me within a week!

This is the final word on queries, cover letters, proposals, and outlines: Every one you send to a potential Buyer must be the best, most finished and polished piece of writing *about* your Product that it can be. Your use of language, your techniques of persuasion, your sense of your Product's marketability, all must be reflected in each carefully constructed sentence. *You must sound as good as you say you are* in order to convince your Buyer to unwrap the package your Product comes in and to give your work a thoughtful and receptive audience.

THE FICTION PRODUCT

I suggest to all novice fiction writers that the best proposal is one chapter with a cover letter explaining that the completed manuscript is available on request. It doesn't have to be the first chapter, only the best one; if it is not the first, a brief foreword may be necessary to explain the plot and identify the characters in the excerpt. With this plus a narrative outline of succeeding chapters, an interested Buyer can make a decision as quickly as it takes him to read the rest of the book, and he can minimize his risk by knowing what he's getting without spending any money. With an unknown writer, he's accepted enough risk already.

Completing a first draft of a novel before attempting to sell it is as important for the writer as it is for the Buyer. The beginning of a novel is like the first week of a love affair; you *know* there's a happy ending coming. But the process of writing a novel is like romance; sometimes, no matter how hard you work at it, it just isn't going to hold up. At which point you're in the embarrassing position of having to return your advance, try to rework your manuscript for another Buyer, and admit to anyone who doesn't already know it (publishing is a *very* gossipy business) that you sold something you couldn't deliver.

If you've already sold one piece of fiction, that is no guarantee that you'll sell your next. Your publisher may not need or want it, regardless of its merits, but he can still be helpful to you in finding someone who does. Every Product you've sold, delivered, and had published is a step up the industry ladder, in terms of widening your perspective, your possibilities, and your connections. So if you've sold your fiction previously, make sure to mention that in your cover letter. If you won prizes, sold subsidiary rights, gotten great reviews, or had any other measurable success (beyond actually selling it, which is plenty to crow about in today's competitive book market), don't hesitate to inform your Buyer. At this stage you can neglect to mention that there are still 4000 copies of the original printing of 5000 in your last Buyer's warehouse, or that a leading critic wrote that reading it made him sick to his stomach. If your Buyer is really interested in your proposal, he'll make it a point to find out the bad as well as the good.

If you've published anything prior to making this Buyer contact, say so, even if your credits are in nonfiction or appeared in periodicals. If you have not published, lead with the theme or subject of the book. Describe your work the way a salesperson might in persuading a book-seller to stock it, or as an editor must to the house's sales reps. Eliminate the subjective, nondescriptive adjectives; use words that accurately portray the type and style of book you've written. Instead of "thrilling" or "sexy" use "gothic" or "erotic"; instead of "hilarious," say "a comic novel."

This was part of my cover letter and proposal for my first novel: "I am an author and journalist who has published three nonfiction books and several magazine and newspaper articles. . . . *Tradeoffs* is a novel about three successful women who share a brownstone in New York City, about their achievements and failures as they struggle to find a balance between personal and professional happiness. . . ." In writing the proposal for that book, I ignored what I've just told you: *Tradeoffs* was only an idea and a ten-page sample at that point. In the eighteen months between selling it and completing it, I often had real doubts about my ability to finish a credible book. So at times did my publisher, editor, and agent. My second novel was finished in first-draft form before I sold it, not because a publisher would not at that point take a chance on me without seeing the entire Product, but because as a writer I wanted to be certain I could do what I set out to accomplish. That level of confidence as well as the performance of my first novel (which was generally quite good in terms of sales, reviews, and subsidiary sales to reprinters and book clubs, but not enough to make me a superstar) made it easier for me to sell because I had a Product I believed in.

Other fiction, such as poetry and short stories, requires a complete manuscript and demands an explanatory cover letter, however brief. For novels, if the Buyer is a stranger to you, a cover letter, sample chapter, and outline should suffice (unless otherwise stated by the Buyer). If you are sending any more than two or three pages, a stamped, self-addressed envelope for return is always recommended by editors.

SASES

Frankly, the whole question of self-addressed, stamped envelopes (SASEs) is a murky one to me. I never send an SASE with a query letter or proposal, but I do when a manuscript of some heft and length is involved. My attitude is that the publisher is a business and I'm a supplier, and the publisher should spend the cost of one stamp to respond to me. But other professionals in the business disagree, so take my behavior as an attitudinal guideline, not an absolute policy, for I suppose if a publisher gets hundreds of manuscripts each year, each of which costs a few dollars to return, he has a right to demand an SASE.

MULTIPLE SUBMISSIONS

Another area of frequent disagreement between writers and Buyers is that of multiple submissions. Buyers don't like it and we do. I think multiple submissions are necessary and proper; from a writer's point of view, the worst thing that could happen is that several Buyers will express interest simultaneously, and you will be in the not unpleasant position of having to choose among them. It is probably wise not to state directly in your cover letter that what you are enclosing has been submitted elsewhere simultaneously, but you can and probably should imply it.

FOLLOW-UP

I am a strong believer in the follow-up. Sometimes it's very direct; a brief, professional phone call after the proper interval of time has passed without a response to your query or proposal from your Buyer. The length of that interval varies; one month is usually more than enough time for a magazine proposal, and two to three months for a book proposal. When you have properly directed your proposal to a *named* Buyer, the follow-up phone call is easy enough to accomplish: "I sent you a manuscript about a paraplegic juggler on June 1 and it is now August. Can you tell me what your response to it was?" Sometimes it may not have been received, or the Buyer was away, or it just slipped to the bottom of his "in" basket. Editors are not offended by a courteous call or even a note asking for a response that has been too long delayed—as long as you don't scold them for delaying it. In any case, a gracious reminder is not sufficient reason for a Buyer to reject your proposal and punish you for your pushiness. No follow-up call or letter has ever prejudiced a marketable proposal or manuscript.

SOME WORDS ABOUT REJECTION

If your proposals, queries, or manuscripts have been rejected by more than five Buyers, it is most likely because the writing is not good enough to explicate the subject or idea; the subject or idea is inappropriate for the Buyer; or both.

Let's take these one at a time. "The writing is not good enough" is a tough one. Some people are just not writers, but no one has been honest enough to tell them that—not their spouse or their best friend or their mother, anyway, who are usually the persons they ask for an opinion. Some editors do send deceptively kind rejection letters, however, and it is the well-meaning among these who do the novice writer the greatest harm by offering hope when none really exists—at least, not for the Product in hand. They say things like "I wish we could publish this, but at this time it is not suitable for our list" or "I'm certain that you will have a successful writing career" out of courtesy, when what they should be saying is something just a little softer than what one editor told a client of mine: "What you have done to the English language is a capital crime."

Other editors may offer more substantive criticism even when they are not going to be interested in buying the Product, no matter how good the revision is. Consider editorial advice of this type as a freebie, and take it when revising your Product. If you've read this far, you're probably going to do it anyway, and if you're really determined, you can probably turn yourself into a competent if not brilliant writer. However, you might want to wait a while before attempting the Great American Novel.

SHOULD YOU PAY SOMEONE TO READ YOUR WORK?

If you are an attentive, objective reader, you're probably the best judge of whether or not your work is good—that is, whether it reflects your real ability. By far the cheapest way to learn to self-criticize your work is to read everything like it in style, tone, and content and compare. It is difficult to earn a living as a writer until you learn to be a good and tough critic of your own work.

It is much easier to be objective about nonfiction than about fiction. If you don't trust your ability to judge your own work, or if you keep getting rejection slips without much substantive criticism in them, you may need a professional critique. The operative word is professional. That means a teacher, a freelance editor, or a published writer. If you have a personal friend in one of those categories, ask him to read your work and, more important, critique it without trying to be polite. Even if you don't agree with his assessment—and unless it's a rave you probably won't—you can learn from the specific criticism that your phrasing is awkward, your plot needs more drama, your characters require further development, etc. Writers who can use feedback intelligently are fortunate. More fortunate are those who know that when feedback is solicited, two different questions are really being asked. One, is it good? In other words, does it hold the reader's interest, please his literary sensibilities, do justice to the idea and theme—does it work? The other, is it salable? Know which question you're asking and ask it of the right person. A creative writing teacher, for example, is not always a good judge of a manuscript's commercial possibilities. The second question would more effectively be put to an editor or agent, someone who knows what the market is buying.

If you pay for a critique of your work, carefully investigate the reader/critic's credentials. Ask for references and check them; find out how other clients did or did not profit from the critic's services. Ask editors who have sought or purchased the work of those clients; most professionals will be glad to supply such references.

Some agents charge for reading and evaluating manuscripts. I firmly believe an agent has no business doing this. Without writers, they'd be out of business, and their professional assessment of whether or not a Product is commercial is the investment they should make in their own business. Stick with agents who do not charge for this and save yourself the money.

Some may see in your unfinished manuscript the sheen of raw talent; others will recognize a marketable idea and be willing to work with you to develop it for submission to a Buyer. If you do use a professional evaluator, make sure you know exactly what to expect for his fee: a chapter by chapter critique, a detailed plan for improving the manuscript, an ongoing editorial relationship, an appraisal of commercial worth, and so on. Before you get to that stage, however, you should look into the many courses, publications, and other services that can make creating and refining your work easier and more efficient. But, as the authors of *How to Get Happily Published* report, "These can be no more than peripheral aids. The central job—developing your individual style, substance and purpose—demands independent, innovative work."

No professional critique, purchased or offered free of charge, is as useful to a writer as attentive reading—reading for content analysis, reading to compare, revise, adapt, amend, and rewrite your manuscript to equal or surpass what has already been published. The final judgment you must make of your proposal is that it meets these criteria:

- The writing is competent and interesting.
- The Product has commercial appeal.
- The Buyer has indicated an interest in publishing this type of material.
- There is market data to support and reinforce the proposal.
- The proposal indicates your ability to deliver a publishable Product.

If you've done all of this and you're still getting rejection letters, put the proposal in a drawer, wipe up the blood on the floor, and get on with finding another idea to turn into a Product. Years, weeks, or months from now you will take it out again, revise it, and go through the whole process of sending it once again to a carefully targeted list of Buyers—perhaps successfully this time around. Meanwhile, it's Inventory. In my file of published work I have Products that were rejected at least once and sold months or even years later. And in my Inventory I have several proposals and some Products waiting for the right set of circumstances to sell. I think of that Inventory as interest-free savings, and so should you.

FICTION AND OTHER
UNRELIABLE MARKETS

The easiest way to break into the fiction market is to have a respected, successful agent fall in love with your completely written novel and convince a Buyer to take a chance on it. Because that's what the fiction market is—chancy. Buyers can predict with some accuracy what the market will be for a nonfiction book on any given topic, but novels are wild cards. No one knows what makes a novel sell. In the book industry they call it "word of mouth," but in every industry there's a different word for something they can't figure out. I call it voodoo. Somehow the word gets out to a trillion readers that they must have this book, and within a few weeks a previously unknown writer is catapulted into the big time. Or, more typically, three thousand people buy copies of that first novel, two thousand booksellers send them back, the book goes out of print in six months, and the writer finds it very hard to get a contract for another novel.

That's why category fiction is beloved by publishers as well as readers. And why it does, in fact, offer the easiest access for the beginning novelist, especially if he has not been able to attract the interest of an agent. I happen to like some kinds of category fiction. So do plenty of other readers, and many publishers have built empires on the back of just this type of material, despite its lack of literary pretensions. I do not think even a skilled writer can produce category fiction if he adopts a patronizing attitude toward it and assumes, as one writer in my seminar said, that "anybody can write one of those junk romances." Anyone can't. Someone who respects the form, loves to read it, and believes Buyers publishing it perform a necessary service—that person can. If you have no respect for the category, if you believe that only those who move their lips when they read buy and devour category fiction and you're not one of those people, you shouldn't be writing it because your insincerity will come through on the printed page.

Many writers who began by publishing category fiction have found it a good way to develop the connections and the talents to market nongenre work. At the very least, a published category novel indicates to potential Buyers of your other Products that you can put words together in an interesting and competent fashion and that you can deliver a finished work. If you have had impressive or even break-even sales with category fiction, you should not find it impossible to get your other Products evaluated and perhaps purchased, if not by your category Buyer then perhaps by another imprint or division of your publishing house. Similarly, a well-published category novel is often enough evidence of your potential to convince an agent to try to sell your serious literary effort. Be warned, however, that agents, like other Buyers, prefer to stick with a genre that has guaranteed profits rather than help a writer move in other directions. So don't expect either your editor or your agent to jump with joy when you tell them you have a 20,000-word epic poem on the Black Death that is a metaphor for contemporary violence.

Almost every category has its own infrastructure of rules, affinity or support groups, and publications, from tip sheets to special-interest writers' conferences. In the same way you would research other markets and Buyers, you should gather as much information as you can about the category you're attempting.

What makes a genre book different from any other novel? Length (they generally do not run over 80,000 words), simplicity of theme and characters, and a formula plot that involves a hero or heroine who surmounts great obstacles, all of which are inherently dramatic, and ultimately triumphs over these roadblocks to happiness or success.

Attentive reading of available titles in your chosen category is an absolute necessity for category writers. All the guidelines written by editors cannot be as useful to you as careful analysis of every successful book in your area. I suggest to category writers that they make content analysis charts of every book they read, indicating similarities and differences in plot, structure, and character.

Category books offer good opportunities for original paperback publication, particularly when they feature a main character who could be used again and again in a series, especially in a mystery, adventure, or science fiction series.

Genres in category fiction change as demographics and cultural and social values change to reflect current realities. As noted under the section "Science Fiction," horror and occult books are now enjoying a vogue which is reflected in the appearance of titles by Stephen King, V. C. Andrews, and others on mass market and hardcover best-seller lists. Within the "Male Adventure" category, a new subgroup of "survivor" books seems to be emerging in much the same way the occult genre developed from science fiction.

The best way for a novice to enter the category market is not by attempting to create a new category, but by spotting trends and establishing an early position in the newest ones, where the competition is not as great and the trend may just be emerging. Here are some genre categories and a brief description of current trends in each one.

THE ROMANCE NOVEL

This kind of category fiction has enjoyed the biggest sales increase in publishing history. An entire new industry has been created to cater to the individual tastes of romance readers. The market has been very tightly narrowcast, and in recent months many new lines have been introduced. Romance subcategories feature and include adult and erotic titles, inspirationals, historicals like Regency romances, young adult novels, ethnics, and illustrated books. Almost every publisher offers formal guidelines for writers detailing appropriate themes, characters, settings, and plots for its romance lines.

SCIENCE FICTION

This genre has long had fascination for a dedicated cadre of readers. In many cities there are specialty bookstores that carry only science fiction titles, though the horror and occult variations on this theme have begun to occupy an increasingly larger amount of their shelf space. Buyers of purer versions of the form are attempting to meet a big public demand for fantasy and speculative writing rather than space invaders or *Star Wars* scenarios: Benign elves, fairies, and other little people are enjoying a current vogue. Arthurian legends retold in a fresh fashion and plots having to do with time travel and ESP are also popular right now among Buyers.

Science fiction editors read anthologies and magazines looking for new writers, so publishing speculative short fiction in outlets like *Analog* is a good way to attract the attention of a potential Buyer. A sample of any published pieces should be enclosed with your first three chapters and a detailed outline of the remainder of your book. Many science fiction editors buy titles in blitzes and then do not purchase again for several months; a big science fiction publisher like Berkley Publishing Group publishes fifteen titles a month, however, so there is almost always an available Buyer for well-written material.

WHITHER THE WESTERN?

Western fiction continues to sell, though publishers keep forecasting the end of the category. What has kept the genre alive is the new so-called adult western, heavily dosed with sex and violence. Some new western lines feature women heroines; publishers are trying to attract new readers to this category, and manuscripts slanted toward women readers are currently in demand by a select few publishers. One reason that the western category seems to be shrinking in terms of total number of titles is the thin line between the classic western and the newer male adventure—these books are often distinguishable from each other only by their settings.

MALE ADVENTURES

These novels may cross the line between thrillers and spy novels, since all feature a tough, macho hero, a villain who is often a foreigner, and a great deal of sex, raunch, and violence. Worldwide's The Executioner series provides a good example of this genre. Most publishers of male adventures also offer tip sheets and writer guidelines.

MYSTERIES

Mysteries may combine some elements of male adventure books, but they are more commonly divided by sub-category: police procedurals, spy stories, horror and occult books that are not truly science fiction, detective novels, capers, and international adventures. Mysteries range from the very sexy to the practically prim, and continue to earn regular sales among a devoted coterie of readers. They are often the only category novels reviewed by prestigious book reviews like the *New York Times Book Review*. Some exceptionally well-wrought mysteries can and do attract a large enough general audience to make the best-seller list; John le Carré and Robert Ludlum have transcended the category in this manner, and have been published in hardcover originals from an early point in their careers.

CHILDREN'S BOOKS

At least a third of the participants in my seminars are children's book writers. Some have a natural talent for the form and an affinity for the market, but many, I think, are attracted to this category because the books look so deceptively easy to create. In fact, writing children's books is very difficult, and cracking the markets within this group can be almost impossible, especially in picture books and other preschool materials. The blend of text and illustrations must be absolutely perfect, and many publishers of children's books prefer to work with teams of writers and artists whose work they know and can depend on.

Some years ago, publishers wanted only children's books that were suitable for use in schools as well as purchase by parents. Now the marketing target has changed, and editors are requesting books that kids themselves can buy with their own rapidly increasing disposable incomes. What is currently desired by children's book publishers is realistic fiction, particularly for the eight- to twelve-year-old reader and for the young adult aged twelve to sixteen. They want fiction that depicts the way children really live today, a generation after the demise of the nuclear family with its male breadwinner, nonworking mother, family dog, and suburban house. Mysteries, adventure, and comedies aimed at this group of younger readers are also in demand.

Young adult fiction is already a subcategory in the romance genre. Sometimes these books cross the line into the children's market and occasionally move from there to attract a wider audience of readers of all ages. Judy Blume's fiction for young adults is read by as many mothers as daughters, according to her publisher. S. E. Hinton's novels, perennially popular with teenagers, have been adapted for the screen by no less an artist than Francis Ford Coppola, and are also moving beyond the traditional limits of young adult fiction into the general market.

Finally, packagers are moving into the children's market with series. If you can create a Product with series potential, you can practically retire. The Children's Book Council (67 Irving Place, New York, NY 10003) publishes complete and careful bibliographies of children's books as well as "Writing Books for Children and Young Adults," which offers tips for writers. *The Children's Media Market Place* is a biennial directory that lists dozens of resources, including periodicals, book clubs, and television and radio stations in the market for youth-oriented materials, and is available in most libraries.

Textbook publishers need materials not covered in the general children's book market, and how-to books for younger readers in areas such as crafts, science, computers, and self-care are a small but important market segment. Many children's book clubs as well as mass market publishers are looking for original books in these areas.

There are some agents who specialize in children's books and keep abreast of trends in this fast-changing market. Like any other category or special market, children's literature has its own rules, organizations, information sources, conferences, and materials. You will find an Information Ozone specific to this market in the ways already described as well as through your usual market research practices among Buyers and Customers. The Children's Book Council reports that children's books "are increasingly classified and specialized, and must fit into publishers' marketing programs to be published by all." The industry feels that the baby-boom generation, which is now raising its own children, will dramatically affect the market in the near future; these couples are generally older than other first-time parents, are more financially established, and are interested in a wide array of educational materials for their kids.

If you have written and illustrated a children's book, by the way, do not ever send original art with your proposal or manuscript. A photocopy of your drawings is sufficient, especially since most publishers prefer to choose their own illustrators. If you are visually artistic as well as verbally skillful, be aware that the test of your children's book is that it must be valid and readable on its own merits; illustrations may help illuminate the text, but they cannot make up for weak writing, plot, or character.

SHORT STORIES

The publishing future for short stories took a decided upturn when more publishers began issuing them in trade paperback form. That does not mean that it is easy to sell a collection of short stories; next to poetry, I think it's the hardest sell in the market today. (And I'm not even going to talk about poetry because that's something you do for love, not money, and lots of luck to you.) Though publishers would deny it, most only sign a short story writer when they think he has the makings of a novelist. This is an area where magazine publication helps a great deal, but still cannot ensure success. Also, it is even harder for a writer of short stories to get an agent than it is to find a Buyer; like publishers, agents know they'll rarely get rich on short stories, and if they do agree to represent you, they'll be pushing you to write a novel. Very few trade publishers will risk more than a token advance, if that, on a book of short stories if the writer has not previously published in one of the few prestige showcases like *The New Yorker, Atlantic,* or one of the very good small magazines. The best credentials for a writer aspiring to publish a book of short stories are a good file of published work, winning one of the major prizes such as the *Atlantic First,* and making the right connections at a writers' conference, especially one that requires juried acceptance like Bread Loaf. And it wouldn't hurt to have a good sample for a novel, either. There are Buyers in this market, but the allocation of money to this segment of their list is small and the competition is very keen.

SELLING SHORT FICTION TO MAGAZINES

There are three kinds of magazines that publish short stories. The first is the large, well-known consumer magazines that devote a portion of their editorial space to short stories. They range from the women's monthly magazines to journals such as *The New Yorker, Atlantic, Harper's, Playboy, Esquire,* and the rest. They pay well, take about sixty percent of their material from agented submissions, and their fiction reflects the general values of or issues of concern to the magazine's audience. Every story that comes into the slicks is read, and editors often add words to printed rejection letters to encourage writers whom they find promising. Some may ask to see other samples of your work if the piece under consideration intrigues them; others who think your work is good but not for them may suggest other possible markets. For most short story submissions, a cover letter should be very brief, stating any published credits you have and a one- or two-sentence description of the topic so that busy editors at magazines with particular requirements can weed out those deemed unsuitable for their readers.

I've found that most magazine editors in the short fiction department are very likely to encourage someone whose work they find promising, and just as quick to reject with a printed letter and no sign of encouragement those works they find of no merit. If your story keeps being rejected with faint praise, keep at it. Most editors will not work through major editorial problems with short stories, so you'll have to follow up such rejections with homework of your own, trying to discern what's wrong with your work and how you can fix it.

One new and promising mass periodical market for short stories is the PEN Syndicated Fiction Project, which functions just like a magazine Buyer, purchasing appropriate stories and syndicating them to participating newspapers. It is funded by the National Endowment for the Arts to encourage practitioners in the field. This revival of a trend—newspaper publication of short fiction—that last saw the light of day in the Twenties is to be welcomed by writers.

The second category is specialty magazines, including what used to be called the pulps: mystery, western, and science fiction magazines. They offer great opportunities to beginning writers, especially since book editors in those fields regularly peruse the specialty magazines in search of talented new writers.

Many magazines aimed at the teenage or young adult market also publish short fiction. Again, book editors in this market find promising new writers through this vehicle and often publish anthologies of short fiction which can earn the writer dividend checks for work already purchased and paid for.

The literary magazines make up a third avenue for magazine short story writers. Characteristically, the pay scale has nothing to do with the quality—or perhaps it has everything to do with it because it often seems that the higher the literary value of the Product, the less a writer is paid for it. Still, publication in literary magazines of merit is often impressive to editors of slicks and also to book publishers, so do not neglect this market if you have the talent to crack it. The rewards can be much greater than the immediate financial return.

11

AGENTS, LAWYERS, AND OTHER SMALL PRINT

AGENTS

In seven years I have had three agents, and I can only say that each relationship represented what Alexander Pope said of remarriage: the triumph of hope over experience. I moved from one agent to the next not because any of them failed to represent me decently and honorably, but because my needs as a writer changed as my markets evolved. At a time when I was writing frequently for magazines, I needed an agent capable of selling to periodicals; later when I needed the services of a film agent, I moved to an agency with a strong presence in that market. With each new publishing experience I gained more understanding of how agents do, or should, work on a writer's behalf.

Yes, that's right—agents work for writers, not vice versa. Often it is difficult to remember this, particularly when you're prostrate with gratitude to an agent for accepting you as a client. Beginning writers usually relate to their agents like children to their parents; they expect them to do everything, to be the sole agent of their happiness. This is an unrealistic expectation, and when an agent-writer relationship is based on it, it is likely to be a brief and unhappy one.

There is no mystery about getting an agent. Almost every one listed in *LMP* will at least respond to a query letter. Some will even agree to look at your work, especially the hungry ones. If it's good enough, if it has commercial or literary appeal, if the agent thinks he can sell it, he'll agree to represent you. Some agents ask for contracts, or at least letters of agreement, with their clients. Most offer a thirty-day to three-month period to break such a relationship, but actually the contract an agent executes for you, which says that all money paid you for a specific Product is to be paid through him, serves as the legal instrument between author and agent.

An agent's value to you is directly related to his or her connections and relationships with Buyers—publishers and editors. Access is the key word; how much access to, attention from, and clout with publishers a particular agent has is an indication of his value. It may not be great if your agent works or lives anywhere except in New York or, particularly in films and television, in Los Angeles. Agents make deals with publishers they know in a market whose trends, needs, and problems change regularly, and the Information Ozone rarely gets beyond the New York skyline except via the trade press, which more often reports what has happened than what is going to happen. So I strongly urge writers to limit their search for an agent to those two cities, except in the unusual circumstances of an agent who was formerly in the publishing capital and keeps up contacts or may even "scout" for a particular house or editor.

The agents who deal with publishers and editors, in person, are the agents you want. The ones who make big deals for superstar writers are the A list of agents. The next echelon is a group of hard-working agents with a decent if not dazzling record of sales for their clients, a group which is respected by publishers and gets the work of their clients reviewed. Many on this B list are much better for a beginning writer because they will take the time, more often than the superagents, to help you develop a proposal and tailor it carefully to the right Buyer. They also tend to be more interested in helping you develop a career as a writer; after all, you may be their next superclient!

It is the C list of agents from whom the beginning writer will most often receive attention. (By the way, agents are nowhere identified on these imaginary lists—they are my own subjective categorizations, but that doesn't mean they aren't real!) These are frequently sole practitioners with small offices; many were formerly editors at publishing houses; some were (and are) writers. They have at least a nodding acquaintance with the industry and usually know the middle level of editors personally.

Now, theoretically any agent can submit your work to any editor at any publishing house, and it will get some attention and be at least several steps ahead of the slush pile of unagented submissions. The A list of agents can always get their clients' work seen by the editors who have power to acquire what they want. Although they must still justify their acquisitions to the editorial board at their house, these editors can buy pretty much on their own authority with relatively high limits on how much they can spend.

Perhaps the best agent a beginning writer can have is a C agent in an A agency—a young, bright, hard-working person who is ambitious and can, with a little effort, get your work to the top editors simply because it comes bearing the submission seal of a respected agency. Also, the resources of a larger agency can be helpful; most small one-person shops do little or no magazine representation, while the larger agencies employ someone just to service the magazine business of their book clients. The economics of agenting magazine work are not favorable; why waste time for ten percent of a thousand-dollar fee, when the same effort on a book would yield a much larger commission? Some of my agents have had magazine reps who have been helpful to me, especially in getting my proposals submitted to new markets. But most of the magazine agents are really only biding their time until they can handle books and films.

Larger agencies are also more efficient in selling your adaptable manuscripts to Hollywood; they either have branches of their offices there or have correspondent relationships with theatrical agents on the West Coast. If writing for films or selling your books to Hollywood is your goal, you would probably be better served by a junior agent at a large agency specializing in films than by a sole practitioner in a strictly literary agency.

This is not to imply that any good literary agent can't sell your work to the movies or television. It is, again, a matter of connections: The better and closer the ties are between your agent and the Hollywood Buyers, the more likely it is that your book will be actively marketed to those Buyers.

What an agent can do for you is represent you and your project to appropriate Buyers, negotiate a contract for you, and act on your behalf to enforce contract provisions and collect your money—for ten percent. Some agents have raised their commissions to twelve and even fifteen percent; my personal feeling is that there are many excellent agents on the A, B, and C lists who will do it for ten, and that should be your goal. But if the chemistry is right between you and someone who charges more, and you feel good about the relationship and what the agent can do for you, go ahead with the higher-priced agent and don't make your decision on dollars alone. The fact is that the amount charged is not an indication of how effective the agent is. And effectiveness is easily measured—how much does he sell for you?

What an agent will rarely do is devise a real marketing

package for your Product; that you must do yourself. Once more, consider what the agent must have to sell to the Buyer—a package with a strong marketing rationale, a well-researched proposal, a solid creative sample. Having a good idea or a good sample is not enough, and most agents will not do your homework for you. They will not have researched your markets, they may not even have a clear idea of how your Product differs from or is like others already available or in process. The more you arm your agent with good selling tools, the more likely he is to make a sale on your behalf.

The important thing to know about any agent you consider (or who considers representing you) is the kind of work he specializes in and the size of the contract he typically negotiates. It won't do you a great deal of good to be represented by an agent who routinely negotiates million-dollar deals if your contract is going to bring in ten thousand dollars; the special relationships that agent has with Buyers will more often be employed on behalf of his big clients than they will on yours. Again, it's simply a matter of allocation of time and resources—if you had a client with a million-dollar book placed with an editor at a certain house and another book with the same editor, same house, at only a fraction of that, where would you put your energy?

Of course, most agents would deny that they treat clients differently depending on the fee they receive for efforts on their behalf. But in the real world, that is what happens. It doesn't matter, of course, if you happen to be the million-dollar client, but it can make a big difference if you're not. If your present and potential income represents just enough to cover your agent's petty cash each month, don't expect him to perform for you in the same manner he would for a client whose commissions cover his overhead and also bring in a profit, no matter how much he believes in your work and loves it. Once he's able to command big advances for you, you'll discover that you're getting the kind of service you want. Which is why I believe that a hungry agent who believes in you is better than a very successful A-list agent, someone who has big-money clients and who may sacrifice your interest to theirs, even (and usually) unintentionally.

As I've said elsewhere in this book, an agent is not always necessary for a nonfiction writer because often the idea can sell the book and samples will indicate whether the writing will be up to par. For the novelist, however, an agent is important; most unagented general fiction never gets past the slush-pile reader. Genre or category fiction does get read and evaluated without an agent's imprimatur because most of it comes in over the transom and houses that publish it have special staffs to deal with that material. If you have managed to elicit a publisher's interest and do not have an agent, you'll probably be able to get one with no difficulty; almost no agent would turn away ten percent of a contract that required no more effort than negotiating and closing a deal. If you are in this fortunate position and feel that you want an agent negotiating for you, don't make his job impossible by agreeing to or even discussing any financial arrangements with your publisher. And if you don't know where or how to find an agent, ask that interested publisher to recommend one. This may seem like a conflict of interest, but it doesn't work that way; your publisher will suggest someone he knows to be honest, capable, and experienced in the kind of writing you're selling.

THE LAWYER

In many cases, the services of a capable lawyer will be easier to engage and cheaper to pay for than those of an agent, particularly if your deal with your Buyer is relatively typical and straightforward. Remember that while your interests and those of your agent (and Buyer) are not always the same, those of you and your lawyer ordinarily are. Of course, it would seem that the former is true—after all, agents work for a percentage of the deal they negotiate for you—but that is not always the case. If, for example, your contract says that you will receive your payment over a two-year period, yet your agent takes his total commission in one big lump out of the first portion of your advance, that is not necessarily in your best interests.

Lawyers usually charge an hourly fee based on the actual work done on your behalf. Even if you have an agent, it is wise to also pay a lawyer to look over your contract, even if he takes no part in the negotiations. Sometimes he will catch clauses in the contract that your agent tells you are "standard boilerplate," and his intercession with your agent, if not your Buyer, can amend those clauses in your favor.

If you engage a lawyer to do the actual negotiating for you as well as check the fine print in your contract, make sure that he has had some experience with publishing contracts. The reliable family lawyer who drew up your will, handled the sale of your house, and got your accident settlement is not necessarily the right person to handle your literary business. Unfortunately, most lawyers with that kind of experience are located in New York or Los Angeles; book contracts are not usual fare for attorneys outside of the publishing mainstream. So talk to other writers in your community and check out their lawyers, or explain to your family attorney why you want a specialist and ask him to recommend one.

THE CONTRACT

Neither agents nor lawyers are necessary in the negotiation of magazine contracts, which are generally straightforward and easy to understand. Still, even magazine contracts use terms and phrases that may be difficult for you to understand, so ask your Buyer to clarify whatever seems unclear to you or check the language carefully

yourself. Here is a brief guide to the kinds of rights negotiated in most magazine and book contracts.

First serial rights (U.S., North America, or both) are
generally sold to magazines or newspapers and give the
Buyer the right to be the first publisher of the material in
the market included therein.

Second serial rights give the Buyer permission to publish a manuscript (or a portion thereof) that has already
been published in either a book or a periodical. (In books,
first serial usually refers to an excerpt published in a
periodical before publication of the entire book; second
serial refers to excerpts appearing after the book's publication).

Foreign serial rights are those sold to markets outside of
North America. If your contract gives a magazine first
serial rights without any qualifying phrase, such rights
may belong to your publisher, so always make sure the
qualifying phrase is in your contract or letter of agreement.

Syndication rights permit a Buyer to publish your book
or article or excerpts from either in several installments in
more than one newspaper or periodical. Simultaneous
rights permit the publisher of several periodicals to use
your material in more than one at the same time or are
rights sold simultaneously to two or more publishers with
different circulations.

One-time rights are just what the name implies, the
right to use your material one time, in one publication, for
one fee. All rights are easy to understand, too, and you
should probably never sign a contract which gives them to
a publisher, since this means that you have lost your right
to sell any part of that work to someone else, or even to
have it anthologized or used in another context without
additional payment (except, perhaps, to your original
publisher, that wily devil).

If you are a *writer for hire,* or write for hire by agreement, you sell not only all rights to your work, but the

copyright as well. Some magazine editors ask freelance or independent writers to sign for-hire agreements—don't.

Subsidiary rights refer to rights other than those for book publication: dramatic rights, foreign rights, paperback reprint or book club rights, licensing rights, and serial rights. In book publishing, these rights are usually divided between author and publisher according to an agreed-upon formula. Those rights in which the publisher has an interest—reprint, for example—will usually be negotiated by him and reflected in your royalty statement; those rights that you, through your agent or lawyer, have reserved to yourself will be negotiated by you or your lawyer or agent.

There are sample contracts prepared by several authorities that outline in general terms the typical provisions of a book contract. The Authors' Guild can provide you with its suggested contract and with samples of typical magazine contracts. Caveat emptor, only this time let the seller—that's you—beware. While these reference materials may be informative, they are by no means the last word in contracts. Check with an agent or lawyer before you even begin to negotiate a book contract on your own behalf. You can negotiate magazine contracts or letters of agreement yourself, especially if you sell only one-time rights. Make sure to check with your magazine editor about ownership or split of subsidiary rights such as broadcast or film rights. Some magazines whose material is occasionally purchased by film Buyers have procedures for sale of those rights as part of any magazine contract with a freelance writer.

COPYRIGHT

Many writers express concern that publishers will steal their ideas—use their original proposals to solicit books or articles on the same subject or theme from another writer. This happens in a very small number of cases, and more often with magazines than with book publishers. There is really no way you can protect yourself, especially if what you have shown them and had rejected is only a proposal and not a completed Product.

Under the newly revised Copyright Act, copyright on works prepared after 1977 is obtained automatically when the work is created—that is, when it is written, typed, or recorded in some way, even without registration with the Copyright Office, lasting for the author's life plus fifty years. Registration is not a condition of copyright but may in some cases be a condition of copyright protection or preservation. It is accomplished by paying a filing fee (ten dollars as of this writing) and depositing a copy of the work with the Copyright Office.

If you do not want to go to that trouble, indicate copyright by using the symbol (c) or the word "copyright" or its abbreviation (copr.), the year of first publication or completion, and your name as owner of the copyright. Put this on all copies of your work—every work. If, for instance, you've sold first serial rights for an article to a publisher, the magazine's copyright registration will not protect your rights in that piece as well as a separate copyright on the article itself will. If you omit the copyright notice, there is a remedy: you can add the notice after publication and register with the Copyright Office within five years after publication or completion. Registration presumes that you are the author, and if you haven't registered the copyright, you can't sue for copyright infringement. For nondramatic works, the relevant copyright form is TX; for scripts, sermons, and other so-called dramatic works, apply to the Copyright Office for form PA (Performing Arts); for anything with graphic elements, the correct form is VA (Visual Arts).

Often newspaper reporters who come to my seminars have questions about who owns the copyright to work done while they were employed by a newspaper, particularly reporters who want to use material gathered in the course of doing their jobs for books or movies. Such work is usually defined as "work made for hire," which means that it is made by an employee within the scope of his employment or it is ordered or commissioned for use as a contribution to a collective work, such as a part of a motion picture, a translation, a compilation, etc. This does not preclude copyrighting your work; there is a provision on the copyright form for protecting your rights in it, even though the employer or other person for whom the work was made is considered the author. Exactly what your rights are in a work made for hire is not always clear. I suggest to people with questions of this nature that when the work is created or just before publication they discuss with their employer what is necessary to protect their rights if they plan to write a book using material gathered or published while they were employees. Sometimes employers will be satisfied with a notice in the later work that "portions of this work originally appeared in *The Beekeeper's Newsletter,*" for example.

To protect your proposals and submissions from possible infringement or plagiarism, add the (c) notice. It may restrain unethical publishers from taking your ideas or material and, say, assigning another writer to work on a project you've conceived and outlined.

It is very difficult to prove that a publisher misappropriated your work, i.e., turned down your proposal and then gave your idea to another writer. This is why a (c) should automatically be affixed to every proposal, and if the movie or book or article turns up written by someone else, talk to a lawyer about your rights or cause of action. Many scriptwriters register their scripts with the Screenwriters Guild to avoid difficulties of this nature. So many lawsuits are initiated in film projects by writers who are certain that Buyers stole their ideas that most film Buyers will not even read a proposal until the writer has released them from liability with a document that seems on first reading to sign away all rights to his material. Included in

Chapter 8 is such an agreement, a variation of which will be demanded by any film Buyer reading unagented submissions.

Most writers who are concerned about being ripped off write for magazines, and it is here that the greatest abuses of a writer's work and trust occur. Some magazines that turn down writers' proposals because they think someone else might do greater justice to the material will pay a kill fee or other token amount to the writer who originated the article idea. Others will not and will respond to cries of "You stole my idea" with denials. In most cases, the sum of money (the writer's fee) is hardly worth a lawsuit. It's one of the inequities of writing for magazines, and my advice to writers is to accept it as a hazard of the trade and get on with the next project. Better yet, come up with a new angle on the subject and use the article that you didn't sell (and someone else wrote) as an indication to another Buyer that there is expressed interest in the subject.

Some magazines routinely assign the same story to several writers. There is nothing you can do about this either, except hope that yours is the best and demand a kill fee and repayment of any expenses you incurred in completing the work. As one writer put it, "I look on submissions to these magazines as contest entries." Of course, no magazines publicly announce that they do this sort of thing, but if you're tuned in to the periodical Information Ozone and make it a point to meet writers who publish in many magazines, you'll learn which ones they are.

Agents, like editors, come in two categories: those who sell and those who edit before they sell. I've had both kinds. My first agent functioned like an editor. He helped me turn an article into a book, and this book, appropriately, is dedicated to him. Other agents have accepted my drafts or proposals and suggested a few minor changes before submitting them for sale. I have had editors who made only minimal changes in my manuscripts and disappeared from the universe on publication day, never to be heard from again unless my work provoked a lawsuit. I've had other editors who loved words as much as publishing lunches; those who actually did hands-on line editing and were involved in the Product at every stage from acquisition to publication . . . and then disappeared from the universe the day after the book was shipped to stores. I've had Buyers who purchased my work and used only the idea, not the Product, like one who paid me for a magazine proposal and asked another, more qualified writer to turn it into a Product. And I had a television Buyer once who paid me a lot of money for a book and used only the title and a few anecdotes from the manuscript, but never sought my opinion or participation in shaping the film. If you are, as they say in Hollywood, "good with a concept," this may happen to you. If it does, use the money they pay you for your idea to subsidize you while you turn the next one into a Product. And if you're so much in love with your own prose that you'd kill your mother rather than see a word of it changed, find another business.

A FEW LAST WORDS
ON BEING A
PROFESSIONAL WRITER

Cultivating professional work habits cannot make you a better writer, as I've told you. But it can make the creative process more efficient, increase the size of your fees and advances, and present you to Buyers as a writer who can give them what they want, can sell, and, in the process, can make their lives easier all around. And a professional Product, even if it's not purchased, can elicit a Buyer's request to see more of your work.

While Buyers say they love to find and nurture new talent, the truth is they'll take a seasoned professional over a raw genius any time. Geniuses are notoriously difficult to do business with, and that's what writing is—a business.

Professionalism starts before you even begin to shape an idea into a Product; it begins with the way you organize your files, keep up with your industry, and make the all-important connections within it. So I'm not going to tell you about keeping an up-to-date Rolodex, getting an ac-countant, choosing a letterhead, or getting a business license. If you don't know how to do those things, get a good book that tells you. Instead, I'd like to say a few words about attitude.

A professional attitude is based on this view of the writing world: You are a business person with a Product and service to sell. Your skill as a writer is part of what you have to offer a Buyer; your interpersonal skills, whether communicated in person or through the written word, are part of it, too.

While this attitude can and should inform your Product, it must be reflected in your business practices. Every contact you make with every Buyer you approach should reinforce the primary communication message: You know your business. What you don't know about it you can learn by thinking intelligently and going to the right source for more information. That source may be a textbook on the right format for a screenplay or the development of a plot line, or it may be someone who's experienced in the publishing industry. Although I have shared some of my sources with you in this book, they will not all be appropriate for every writer; your own interests, inclinations, and markets will help you find your own.

This same level of professionalism is central to career planning. Writers' careers don't just happen, any more than those of other professionals do. Each Product you sell must return your investment in more than just money; it should bring you more industry connections, widen your potential markets, do credit to your ability, enhance your reputation, and lead to another sale.

Thus you cannot always judge an assignment or contract on strictly financial terms. Sometimes it may be rewarding because it puts your work in front of a different audience, increases your learning curve, or makes an impact on your world and its inhabitants. There are many ways to get from where you now are as a writer to where you want to be. Some may demand moving from a special to a general market or vice versa; others may require you to develop proficiency in a different medium. Or it could be that you will have to take a detour—into independent or self-publishing, for instance—in order to arrive at a goal you now may be able to sense only dimly. Each move presents new opportunities, though they may not turn out to be those you envisioned at the beginning.

Setting goals and implementing them became part of my professional attitude after I had interviewed successful executives for two books (proof that writing does, indeed, teach you what you need to know). All successful professionals have this in common: They consider where they want to go, and how they can get there, with each new project, assignment, or opportunity. If you are a good writer, professionalism can help you be a selling one. And professionalism is essential if you hope to turn your writing into a decently paying career.

If you consider yourself a professional, you'll think, act, and write better. And you'll discover the enormous opportunities that exist for writers—to grow and learn in your career, your Craft, and, yes, your Art. (Deep down, you see, I care about Art, too. Most of all. Shouldn't every writer?)

Good luck. It's a great job, and you can get it.